A GUIDE TO THE

SUPREME COURT

A GUIDE TO THE

SUPREME COURT

DOROTHY A. MARQUARDT

THE BOBBS-MERRILL COMPANY, INC.
Indianapolis / New York

Designed by Dan Kirklin
Manufactured in the United States of America

Second Printing

Library of Congress Cataloging in Publication Data

Marquardt, Dorothy A
  A guide to the Supreme Court.

  Bibliography: p.
  Includes index.
  1.   United States.   Supreme Court.   I. Title.
KF8742.M37   347'.73'26   76-47338
ISBN 0-672-52168-7

Contents

Foreword

THE SEAL OF THE SUPREME COURT of the United States of America is embossed on writs, judgments, mandates, and other official documents dealing with Court business. Taken from the Great Seal of the United States, it was adopted as the official Court symbol of high authority and power on February 3, 1790.

The Supreme Court is a structure of law designed (and frequently redesigned) to protect the liberties of all Americans and to advance both their private and their public well-being. Over the years, that structure has reached profoundly courageous and wise decisions. These opinions serve to safeguard our democratic heritage, and the Court's continued administration of justice should be protected because of the freedoms enjoyed by all citizens under this guardianship of the law.

In order to cope with the multitude of problems that confront each session of the Supreme Court and that increase with the Court's growth in power, the Justices must have a knowledge of all the facts so that they can exercise careful judgment in decisions which will become fair and equal law. A unity of ideas must finally prevail, with exploration and discussion undertaken by each Justice before a majority vote can be reached and delivered, although the minority opinion (the viewpoint of those Justices who disagree with the decision of the Court) has often had great influence on later cases. The law must be administered without passion or prejudice, and the law must be interpreted, not made, by the Justices of the Court. The integrity and wisdom of the Supreme Court, the interpreter of the rules of government under the Constitution, have always been considered to be the backbone of the nation.

The Supreme Court commands perhaps the most respect of any part of the Federal government. During its history, the nation has been shaped, judicial prestige and respect have developed, and the Constitution has been transformed. The Court has functioned as an organizational body performing a group of related acts and processes. The history of the Court serves as a record which depicts past, present, and future judicial events as steps in the sequence of Court activities, and thereby provides material for the study of the character and significance of each event. This book deals with the function and history of the United States Supreme Court.

Part One

Function and History

Chapter I

The Purpose and Authority

THE SUPREME COURT OF THE UNITED STATES is the highest court in the nation. Its basic function is to act as arbiter of the Constitution, which always has been and shall continue to be the supreme law of the land. The Supreme Court may be viewed as the conscience of the Constitution. The fundamental principles of the nation and of the individual states are protected by the Court. It is the obligation of the Supreme Court to ensure that the national power is exercised in the national interest, as the Founding Fathers intended. One purpose of the Court is to determine the powers and duties of the government and to guarantee certain rights to the people. The Court must provide assurance that the rights of all Americans, regardless of race or creed, are protected; that the accused shall be granted a fair trial; and that our society shall continue to be a democratic one. As long as the Supreme Court remains the living voice of the American Constitution, it will and must say *what* the law is. Today, with widespread criticism of and outspoken contempt for American political life, the Court has had the courage to take concrete action in upholding and preserving the highest ideals of Americanism. We need the Supreme Court today more than ever before, because precious freedoms can be lost

in the constant rush of modern-day enterprise and flexible administration and in the confusion caused by fear of nuclear
disaster.

The architects of the Constitution designated the Supreme
Court to head the Judicial branch of the Federal government.
It is the only Court specifically created by the Constitution. The
Court and the limits of its jurisdiction are provided for in Article III of that document. The real distinction of the Supreme
Court, the third branch of government, lies in its equal rank
with the Executive and Legislative branches. It is the least powerful of the three, however, as it is unable to enforce its own
decisions.

The Court's specific function, to act as supreme interpreter
of the Constitution, permits it to make decisions on petitions,
Federal laws, and treaties. Thus, the highest tribunal in the
United States has established the principle of judicial legislation. The Court has exerted considerable influence on many
crises and problems, righting private wrongs or otherwise alter-
ing life for millions of citizens. When the law is challenged by an
individual or a group, the Supreme Court must determine the
legality of the law. It is the mainstay of American law and justice, the vital stem of the legal system and the protector of
America's liberties.

The high Court determines just what the law is only when
an actual petition comes before it under the fixed rules of procedure. The Constitution permits the Court to settle conflicts
between the states and the Federal government, and to decide
the constitutionality of Executive action. The most important
petitions deal with the laws enacted by the Congress. If the
Supreme Court declares a law to be just and in accordance with
the Constitution, it remains a law. If it declares that a particular
law violates the Constitution, that law is invalidated. The sole
and final power of the Supreme Court to approve or disap-
prove of a law is unequaled in the Western hemisphere. It is a
unique American contribution to political science.

Interpretation of the Constitution and other bodies of law
is often referred to as the process of "judicial review." When
applied at the constitutional level, it affects the basic principles
and traditions of our country. The Court must resolve conflicts

between the supreme law of the land and acts of Congress or of a state legislature. However, this authority is not specified in the Constitution. The power of "judicial review," established in 1803 by Chief Justice John Marshall and exercised ever since by the Supreme Court, was adopted as a necessary power of the Court. Decisions handed down by the high tribunal affect all citizens and reach into every corner of American life. The Court does not give advisory opinions or legal advice, even if requested to do so by the President or the Congress. Every American who cherishes freedom in all its aspects should thoroughly understand the judicial power of the Supreme Court, for it is the power which turns the wheel of justice.

The basic purpose of the Supreme Court is to serve justice by determining what just law is. Just law awards to every man what rightfully is his, and no more. The Court and its business belong to the people. The Supreme Court hands down decisions on cases presented to the Bench by real people with real problems. Its main function, as arbiter of the Constitution, allows the Supreme Court to assign limited jurisdiction to lower courts in its numerous and varied opinions. The Court is the ultimate judicial body which resolves the relentless arguments and bewildering questions that come under its jurisdiction. The supreme law of the Constitution is the deciding authority in such matters of conflict. It is the duty of the high tribunal to attempt to meet the needs and demands of its own times. During riotous and violent periods, the Court is often regarded as a political device and sometimes becomes as involved with economic and political issues as with legal problems. The doctrine of judicial review permits the Supreme Court to strengthen the core of the government and to guarantee respect for individual rights.

The United States is a great and powerful nation; therefore it must maintain a high Court of equal stature. People's property and rights would be endangered if its power were less. The Court is not an end in itself, but its fundamental purpose—to serve justice—makes it the greatest and most powerful tribunal in the world. Most Americans realize how important the Supreme Court is in a democratic society, and they generally respect its decisions. However, the power of the

Court is not always perfect and absolute. If a majority of the people believe a particular Court opinion to be wrong, that judgment can be reversed by the Court itself or by the Congress, or a Constitutional Amendment can nullify a Court decision, but this method is slow and difficult. The Congress usually prefers not to oppose the Supreme Court. Therefore, it is safe to say that the law generally is what the high Court declares it to be. If we, the people, should attempt to amend the Constitution despite the decisions of the President, of the Congress, and of the Supreme Court, the law would become one of whim, and not what the Court has declared it to be. Public esteem and understanding will help the Court uphold the Federal system of government. The conditions and mood of the times, changing membership within the Court, and extreme tensions that are a part of a progressive democracy are all vital in creating changes in Court procedure. The Court has continued to reflect upon and more closely define past decisions that have contributed to the background of Americanism.

The Justices of the Supreme Court cannot be influenced merely by what they personally and individually deem to be correct or wrong in rulings that require Court opinions. They realize the disaster that might occur if they permitted this to happen. The Court has always attempted to promote understanding of its judicial function in American living. As guardian of the Constitution, the high tribunal has powers that include the preservation of individual and states' rights and upholding the supremacy of national laws. Difficulties have sometimes developed between Federal and state governments in exercising control over the same areas of the law; and conflicts in the operation of national government occur among the three branches, namely, the Executive, the Legislative, and the Judiciary. At the same time, their similar outlooks bring them together to guide the nation in times of progress and crisis. As interpreter of justice, the Judiciary has the final authority over actions of the President and over the constitutionality of laws passed by the Congress. Despite this authority, however, decisions of the high Court have often been disputed, its opinions challenged.

Most of the work of the Supreme Court comes under its

appellate jurisdiction, its authority to confirm or reverse the decisions of lower courts. Most cases reviewed by the Supreme Court come from the Federal courts of appeals. In some cases, the high Court reviews the decisions of Federal district courts directly. It also examines the workings of the Federal Court of Customs and Patent Appeals and of the Court of Claims.

Occasionally, the Bench decides to hear a few petitions on cases which have not been tried by another court. Such authority is called original jurisdiction. The Court has this specific power in cases affecting ambassadors and other public ministers and consuls, in disputes between two or more states, and in arguments to which the United States is a party. Such cases compose only a small fraction of the Court's docket.

The Congress established the Federal court system by means of the Judiciary Act of 1789, which included rules governing the Supreme Court. The checks and balances system of the Constitution grants Congress the power to determine both the size and the judicial limitations of the high Court in areas not definitely prescribed in the Constitution. Since the Congress ruled that judicial review was to be granted by the Court only in a few specific cases, the Court was cautious in its selection. However, in 1803 the Court acquired broader power under a new explanation of the judicial review clause of the Judiciary Act. Judicial review was established as a function of the Court by Chief Justice John Marshall in *Marbury v. Madison* in 1803. He declared that if a law enacted by the Legislative branch of government is in opposition to the Constitution, the Supreme Court must base its opinion on the higher body of law, the Constitution. The consistent exercise of constitutional law throughout the country was established by this opinion.

A mood of calmness generally prevails over the Supreme Court, but sudden explosions of feeling can erupt. The forces of conflict in American life frequently result in legal actions that demand impartial decisions being laid before the Court. The opinion of the Court may not please either side and seldom satisfies both. In a sense, the Court is the combat zone for those wanting to initiate or repeal a law. It is especially in this role that the Supreme Court must, according to its constitutional responsibility, hand down decisions that are both legal and fair.

The process of judicial adjustment and compromise has safeguarded individual and national security. Thus, the Judicial branch of government does indeed work and has firmly established its place in American government.

The Supreme Court cannot possibly review all of the cases decided by the lower courts. Because of the heavy workload of the Court, only a few cases, those considered to be of the utmost importance, can be chosen. Most cases reach the Court by way of a writ of certiorari, often simply called a "cert," which means that four out of the nine Justices vote that a petition is important enough to demand Supreme Court review. Whenever the Court accepts a case on cert, it is acting to maintain legal uniformity of the Federal and state legislatures. It would not be fair or proper to do otherwise. The Supreme Court is also permitted to grant certiorari to itself, so that it may review cases of national interest. Each case that comes before the Court for certiorari is reviewed by all nine Justices, who then decide whether the case shall be accepted or denied. The amount of time available to the high Court is limited, and for this reason certiorari must be refused in many cases, even though the Court may well disagree with the rulings of the lower courts. The appellate jurisdiction of the Court gives it the authority to confirm or reverse actions of state legislatures. A variety of other cases occupy the rest of the Court's time.

The major purpose of the Supreme Court, to keep the Constitution of the United States alive and safe, has been carried out throughout American history. Despite its stability, the Court has functioned and will continue to function as an agent of change. It is concerned with the meaning and constitutionality of the law rather than only with the fate of those who confront the law. Without the Judiciary, the United States government would cease to function.

Because of changes in American life which have been brought about by the passage of time and because of recently appointed Justices, new interpretations of the law are bound to occur. During a given period, a Court opinion might have been appropriate and sufficient, but years later that opinion may perhaps demand reevaluation, and a new Court decision may be reached. Both decisions may be intended to serve the same purpose of interpreting the Constitution, but in different eras.

There is no such thing as static justice. The Court's power to examine and give judgment on its own sometimes obsolete opinions is necessary. Such a judicial system was the original intent of the framers of the Constitution, thus making secure America's freedoms, liberties, and rights. In their wisdom they designed a document which is actually only an outline, allowing the Court to insert new decisions to replace outdated ones. If enough people disagree with the Court's ruling in a Federal matter, the Constitution itself can be changed. This has happened several times. Both the Eleventh Amendment (referring to decisions against a state) and the Sixteenth Amendment (establishing the Federal income tax) were passed in order to reverse earlier decisions of the Court. These changes contributed to the growth of the nation and consequently helped to form a practical and efficient government throughout the years. As long as the Judiciary branch of the government exists, so shall justice.

The Supreme Court's power has often been in dispute, but this power, established by the nation's first Judiciary Act of 1789, has never been removed. One of the main reasons for its endurance is the respect which the high Court has always extended to the lower courts. This respect has been preserved by legal procedures and rules made by judges and by the Justices of the Court.

The nation and the world have changed far beyond the original scope of the Constitution. The enormous power that the Supreme Court exercises over the law of the land is earned by the integrity of the Court and upheld by the high regard of the American people. Except for Amendments to the Constitution, during most of its existence the Court has been in complete charge of the basic principles of the law by which we still live. The men who wrote the Constitution foresaw that the original regulations would require change as the country expanded and as time went on, and so a system for making changes, called Amendments, was instituted.

There have been twenty-six Amendments to the United States Constitution since its birth in 1789. The first ten

Amendments, which were all proposed at the same time, are known as the Bill of Rights and have been in force since 1791. The most recent Amendment, adopted during the term of the Burger Court, was proposed and passed in 1971. The Twenty-sixth Amendment states: "The right of citizens of the United States, who are eighteen years of age or older, to vote shall not be denied or abridged by the United States or by any State on account of age." Section 2 of the Amendment says: "The Congress shall have power to enforce this article by appropriate legislation." Amendments to the Constitution have provided new concepts of freedom and further defined the essence of the American way of life, and they have succeeded in protecting the rights of minorities while always depending upon the approval of the majority for support.

There is an awesome quality to the authority of the Court. Basically, it is founded upon trust in the law, the written law of legislatures and the laws resulting from Court decisions. American confidence in the integrity of the rulings of the Judiciary and the universal agreement that the law must be obeyed have helped the Supreme Court work for the good of the people. The most powerful Court in the nation, however, cannot enforce its own decisions. The ultimate power of the law rests on consent to the law, and the power of the Court might cease to exist if its rulings had to be carried out by force.

The Court has been described as the umpire of all great legal problems. It is not above criticism, nor is it exempt from error. As we have seen, Court rulings can be changed. The Court undertakes heavy burdens and becomes subject to attack from those who disagree with its actions. Public criticism of the powers and decisions of the Judiciary has existed since its inception. When it makes a decision, the critics are many. The Supreme Court has never escaped the dissent that is heard when its opinions are announced. No matter how extremely clear-cut the Court's opinion is, a legislative attack is inescapable. Disagreement occurs within the Court and among the Justices more frequently today than in the past. Violent attacks on the Court are often a sign that it is operating properly, in spite of political issues linked with constitutional inquiry. Without criticism, the Court might forget its real function, might evade difficult problems by going along with the flow of popular feeling. Instead, the Court remains alert because of public and professional review and criticism. In any event, the Court lacks the power to endure long amidst popular disapproval. If the Court refuses to approve the Congress's laws, the statutes can be changed. If the interpretation of the Constitution by the Court obstructs needed legislation, the Constitution can be amended. Radical assaults on the Court, including efforts by the Congress to reduce its appellate jurisdiction, have usually been defeated. The Supreme Court has survived many storms, mainly thanks to its own self-imposed correction, examination and scrutiny. Even after a great deal of argument and criticism, most citizens of the United States feel that the Judiciary, whatever its faults, remains the most detached and trustworthy guardian of the nation's liberties.

The Court as we know it will survive only as long as the public continues to accept it as the source of all judicial power. We are living in a period of marked tension and swift social and technological change, characterized by almost constant confusion and doubt. Because of this, the Supreme Court must remain a strong and efficient agent of the law if our free society is to survive. It must administer justice efficiently and effectively, and it must protect the rights of all. The United States government has often been upheld by the action of the Court during critical periods. The Supreme Court has made our nation's growth and preservation, its strength and authority, both feasible and enduring. That the Court can succeed in its basic purpose is a tribute to its integrity, impartiality, and independence. Fully aware that it must not be swayed from its constitutional purpose by popular opinion, turmoil, or pride, the Court has on many occasions set its face firmly against national feeling and prejudice.

From time to time, changes occur in the functions of the Supreme Court and its definitions of the law. National conditions of the times, combined with the economic, political, and social beliefs of members of the Court, are major factors for occasional change. In the beginning, the main purpose of the Court was to deal with controversies between national and state government. In 1789, as already noted, Article III of the Constitution stipulated the original jurisdiction and limitations of the Supreme Court. However, in 1798, the Eleventh Amendment to the Constitution was passed, stating: "The judicial power of the United States shall not be construed to extend to any suit in law or equity, commenced or prosecuted against one of the United States by Citizens of another State, or by Citizens or Subjects of any Foreign State." This simply means that no state may have a legal suit brought against it in a Federal court by residents of another state or of a foreign country. The Eleventh Amendment was the result of a Supreme Court case in which a resident of the State of South Carolina sued the State of Georgia (*Chisholm v. Georgia*) in 1793. The lower court's decision established that a state could be sued by an individual, under the judicial power contained in the Constitution. It was a great shock to the country, for if suits like this were to become a frequent practice, the nation could be pulled apart. The Eleventh Amendment resolved this difficulty. However, the main problem was to determine just when such a legal action becomes an action against a state, without precluding legal action by a resident against his own state. The Court ruled that all such cases would be covered by the terms expressly stated in the Amendment.

Today, the high Court's major concern is to function as protector of individual rights and freedoms in such areas as racial equality (the Court has made many decisions regarding voter registration and school integration), labor (the National Labor Relations Board was made the arbitrator of union activities by the Court in 1959), crime (the 1966 Miranda decision required policemen to warn detained suspects of their right to silence and counsel), obscenity (the First Amendment's guarantees of free speech protect a wide range of material), and welfare (a five-man majority of the Supreme Court ruled that welfare recipients are legally entitled to hearings before their monetary compensations are cut off).

Some of these cases have won the general confidence of the people, while others have produced criticism and resentment of the Court, with resulting demands for changes in the Judiciary branch of government. Chief Justice Warren Burger has reasoned that the Court "should not inflexibly deny to each of the states the power to adopt and enforce its own standards."

And yet, in times of great dissatisfaction with Court rulings throughout our history, many citizens have wanted to reduce the Court's administrative functions, to weaken its legal power, and to restrict its jurisdiction. The majority of the American people have disapproved of such policies and have thereby helped to strengthen the foundation of the Court against efforts to turn the tide of justice. No form of government can be contrived that will be satisfactory to all people at all times. However, it can be safely assumed that, even with all its imperfections, the Court of today does its job far better than any substitute recommended. Its very existence has proved to be a bulwark of security for the United States.

The Supreme Court also must rule on the constitutionality of legal limitations on the individual rights and duties of every American citizen. If the decision of the Court is challenged, the problems may be settled in one of four ways: the law may be changed; the law may be repealed; the Court may change its decision; or the Constitution may be amended.

The Fourteenth Amendment deals in part with the rights of individuals ". . . No state shall make or enforce any law which shall abridge the privileges or immunities of citizens of the United States; nor shall any State deprive any person of life, liberty, or property, without due process of law; nor deny to any person within its jurisdiction the equal protection of the laws." In 1883 the Supreme Court ruled that a certain civil-rights law passed in 1875 was unconstitutional; then in 1896 the Court ignored the Fourteenth Amendment and ruled in favor of segregation. This decision permitted whites to discriminate against blacks and demonstrated total disregard for the equal-rights clause of the Constitution.

In 1954 the Supreme Court ruled segregation unconstitutional, and desegregation became law. In its capacity as the final authority in such matters, the Court has also extended more rights to people on welfare and to people accused of crimes.

In general, the Court has permitted state governments to make and enforce those laws that discriminate among different classifications of people, so long as the grounds for discrimination are reasonable and fair. For example, the Court has maintained that it is reasonable, for tax purposes, to group persons according to their incomes. Also, for educational or welfare purposes, people may be grouped according to their professions or occupations. On the other hand, the Court has decided that people may not be classified by any state government according to their race or religion for any reason whatever. From time to time, the Congress has granted the Supreme Court power to recommend rules of procedure to be followed by the lower courts of the nation. Consequently, regulations announced by the Supreme Court are now in force to guide district courts in the handling of civil and criminal cases, appellate proceedings, bankruptcy transactions, copyright suits, minor criminal offense hearings, and admiralty cases before U.S. magistrates. Prior to 1925 the Supreme Court asserted that the Bill of Rights applied only to the Federal government, but it has since handed down decisions that guarantee that these rights shall apply to the state legislatures as well. Ever since, the rights and liberties of all Americans have been protected against infringement by any law of either Federal or state legislatures.

In the past, governments other than ours have seen a separation of the Executive and the Legislative branches as the best means of controlling the authority of each. In the eighteenth century, no government except the United States had added a third branch to the separation of powers. Before they were able to devise a government divided by law into three separate branches, the Founding Fathers needed many years of experience with other forms, and an understanding of the essential weakness of the two-branch system. Most important, they realized the need for a separate and independent Judiciary in order to maintain a balance between the Executive and Legislative authority and to preserve the division between Federal and state governments, as provided by the Constitution.

Because Justices are appointed, not elected, the high Court of the national government sits aloof and separate from the population and is not subject to the conflicts and political tensions of the other two branches. The Supreme Court not only must be the interpreter of the Constitution and decide on its practical application, but also has to keep abreast of the times and not allow the government's legal procedures to become antiquated and inapplicable to current needs. This involves the tradition of stare decisis, which means that once the Court has established a legal principle by its decision on a case, that principle shall be valid for cases of a similar nature. The Supreme Court usually followed established decisions and policies in its early history. This practice promoted stability and predictability in the law. At the turn of the century, Associate Justice Oliver Wendell Holmes (1902–1932)* strongly deplored the principle of stare decisis. *Stare decisis* is a short form of the legal phrase *Stare decisis et non quieta movere* (to stand by decisions and not disturb settled matters). He was concerned about the force which custom had exerted in the law and about the need to review history in order to undertake a logical study of the law. On the rule of stare decisis he said, "It is revolting to have no better reason for a rule of law than that it was so laid down in the time of Henry IV. It is still more revolting if the grounds upon which it was laid down have vanished long since, and the rule simply persists from blind imitation of the past." The principle of stare decisis was eventually discarded and has little importance in Court decisions today. A choice of principles is now executed by the Court. The rules of the Constitution were designed for the changes of time rather than for one specific era.

Throughout its history the Supreme Court has shaped and reshaped the procedures of constitutional law in our system of government. Attempts by the Court to guarantee complete fairness in all cases that come before it have been a major contribution to our society. The Court can thus develop a pattern of fair play for all other branches of government to follow. Rarely does the Court declare Executive or Legislative action unconstitutional. However, the Court itself—like other agencies of the Federal government—is acutely aware of how far it may go in acting out its constitutional role. Whatever the result of a case, constitutional conflict may focus public attention on moral standards. Public outrage at government policy can result from such controversies. This problem helps remind the Court that American roots remain deeply implanted in its heritage of legal justice.

* Such dates refer to the term in office.

Since the Supreme Court is the umpire of judicial leadership, the other branches of government follow its example. In the past, the high Court has been concerned with questions of the national economy, of interstate commerce, and of government organization. A prominent issue which is before the current Court is the protection of individual rights.

Once it has been handed down, a Court opinion must be supported by exact and specific reasons, principles, and explanation. No other branch of government is required to do this. Once the Supreme Court argument begins, it sometimes accomplishes in one hour or in one day more than a Senate debate accomplishes in a week.

The Court's careful procedures are a testimonial to the Court's ideals. The effects of each decision extend far beyond the case in question. Critics of the Court believe that it does not and cannot function properly because, they say, it lacks awareness of current social and economic problems and has, in fact, lost touch with the moods and needs of the country. Of course the high Court is not always right, but as the final authority on judicial arguments, it must eventually resolve all the bitter legal disputes that confront the nation.

An understanding of the Supreme Court, its design and jurisdiction, its functions and history, can to some degree assure Americans that it is acting in its proper role as the guardian of individual rights and freedoms, and will continue to do so. The Constitution clearly states that it and all Federal laws and treaties are the law of the land; the Supreme Court, as interpreter of the laws, can declare Executive orders and Legislative acts of both the Federal and state governments unconstitutional.

One function of the Court—determining whether laws have violated the aims of the Constitution—has developed gradually with the temper of the times over the years. Consequently, the opinions of the Court have also changed. The Court has reversed its decisions in over a hundred cases during its history.

Because of the lifelong terms of its appointed Justices, the Judiciary is generally inclined to be a nonpolitical part of government, and this has sometimes created friction among the three branches. However, no branch can be severed from the others if the system of checks and balances is to work properly.

Jurists have criticized the Court on the grounds that it operates beyond its constituted purpose. Court decisions are actually not subject to review except by the Court itself; only when a majority of the people disagree with the decision of the Court can the Constitution itself be altered through Amendment. The enactment of a Constitutional Amendment is a way to protect and preserve the liberties of individuals.

Adopted in 1868, the Fourteenth Amendment guaranteed equal protection under the law to all citizens, and judicial legislation was thus begun. It permitted the Court to increase the scope of the Bill of Rights on both the state and Federal levels. Public criticism has abounded during the last two decades, particularly when the Court guaranteed a criminal suspect the right to counsel and ruled that statements made by the suspect during interrogation without counsel could not be used as evidence in his trial. Many people felt that the Court was protecting the criminal (*Escobedo v. Illinois*) rather than the law-abiding citizen. State courts debated the question of whether the Supreme Court thereby made a mockery of state law. Despite harsh criticism of this sort, the high Court has been unequaled in its contribution to civil rights and individual freedom, especially during the 1950s and 1960s.

The Supreme Court was never intended to orbit around the Executive branch of government, even though its members are nominated by the President. As prominent and self-reliant men, appointed with permanent tenure and guaranteed salary, the Justices have maintained their independence beyond the terms and beyond the control of any President. The Court exercises its judgment both as a court of law and as a constitutional court. As a court of law, its purpose is to resolve arguments between specific groups, one of which is sometimes the Executive branch of the government. As a constitutional court, it interprets the supreme law of the land. In both functions, the Court's obligation is to serve the Constitution and justice, and not merely the Executive or Legislative branch. At the same time, it protects the separation of powers by safeguarding our cherished freedom against government actions and preventing either of the two principal arms of government from politically controlling the other. The framers of the supreme law defined the relationship between the Judicial and Executive branches, because they viewed the Congress, especially the House of Representatives, as the most dangerous threat to the constitutional system of the separation of powers.

On a few occasions, the Supreme Court has determined that Presidential actions have not been constitutional. In only a few Court decisions has the authority of the President been in doubt. In 1866 for instance, in *Ex parte Milligan*, the ruling of the Court greatly affected the other two branches of government. Five of the nine Justices declared that neither the Congress nor the President had the power to authorize courts-martial under the conditions present in the case. Chief Justice Salmon Portland Chase (1864–1873), writing for the minority, upheld the power of the Congress. However, the constitutional power of the President has often been upheld by the Supreme Court in broad and positive terms.

In the view of some, the relations among the three branches of government tend to influence judicial decisions. The Congress more than the Presidency has attempted to overturn Court rulings through the process of Constitutional Amendment. In most cases, the Executive branch has defended the Judiciary or remained neutral. In recent years, successful Legislative efforts against Supreme Court rulings have included the 1947 Labor–Management Relations Act and the 1948 Crime Control Act. Usually the Congress has acted against the authority and independence of the Court, but on occasion the Executive has made the effort. President Franklin D. Roosevelt tried to increase the membership of the Court during the New Deal era.

Numerous attacks on the jurisdiction of the Court resulted in legal action in 1869. Following the Civil War, the Congress removed habeas corpus power from the Court, thereby depriving the judicial body of its right to hand down a decision on a petition which questioned Reconstruction legislation (*Ex parte McCardle*). Andrew Johnson, the seventeenth President of the United States, vetoed the Congressional Act, only to have it reenacted by Congress.

Throughout its history, the Supreme Court has been subject to constant attack in an effort to decrease its jurisdiction. In the early decades of the nineteenth century, these attacks involved the Court's authority over state litigation. More recently, during the 1950s, the Congress tried in vain to remove the Court's jurisdiction over various cases, especially those involving national internal security. President Dwight Eisenhower supported the Court. In both instances the authority of the Court to interpret and apply the law was confirmed, thereby reestablishing the basic function of the Judiciary.

Presidents past and present and various agencies of government have learned that they manipulate the Court at their own risk. It is the duty of the Court to fully explore all facets of the case before it, prior to reaching a decision. It is also the duty of the Court, especially when national issues are involved, to bring together the minority and the majority, the high Court and other governmental branches, the nation and the states.

Many parts of the government depend on the Court to deal with politically difficult problems. For example, officials can cope with pressure groups for cleaning up river pollution by saying that it would be impossible to ban the use of a river because the high Court would rule it out. This puts the Court in jeopardy since it appears that the Court is being used as a means of passing the buck on political issues. Usually, the Court has refused to deal with political problems. The high Court is supposed to act as defender rather than enforcer of the law.

The Supreme Court often voices its opinion when public reaction to some difficult situations becomes intense, yet it remains within the boundaries of its limited power. Simple explanations of the Court's ideals and restraints are necessary in order to maintain a free government for a free people. However, its freedom from political control and responsibility makes the Court all the more vulnerable to public criticism. But this keeps the Court abreast of public opinion and provides for the continuity of constitutional law. Hence, the Court serves as a guide in lawmaking, in governing public affairs, and in granting inherent rights and freedoms to all American citizens.

"I'll take this all the way to the Supreme Court!" outraged citizens cry when they feel that they have been cheated by some litigation. To reach the Supreme Court, a petition must involve a constitutional question or some other basic principle of law. The high tribunal will often impose restraints upon itself to avoid handing down too many constitutional rulings. For example, the Court may refuse to examine such cases on the basis that no constitutional grounds exist, or the Court may refuse either to agree or to disagree on a decision which is not disputed by one of the parties involved. When an act of Congress is being debated, the Court will attempt to avoid conflict by seeking an explanation for Legislative action. The Supreme Court must exercise discretion in the selection of cases to be heard, since each year more than 4,000 civil and criminal petitions are filed for debate. Congress has provided for regular and special courts to hear and settle most cases, so as to reduce the workload of the Court. However, when every other possibility of appeal in a case involving a Federal dispute has been exhausted, it is up to the Supreme Court to review the decisions of the lower courts.

Our ideal of equal justice under law has become a living truth in recent years, largely because the principles derived from decisions of the Supreme Court have emphasized individual freedom for members of all classes of society. Major examples include Court decisions requiring nondiscrimination and integration in all parts of American life. Only if the Court continues to enlighten and educate the people will its deliberations guarantee the rights of every citizen in America. It must be a system that "comes home in its effects to every man's fireside: it passes on his property, his reputation, his life, his all," remarked the fourth Chief Justice, John Marshall (1801–1835).

Chapter II

The
Daily Routine

SINCE 1935, THE COURT has done its work in a permanent home in Washington, D.C. The Supreme Court Building is a white marble structure whose elegant and ornate Corinthian columns and other features modeled on Greek architecture blend well with the Capitol directly facing it and with the other government buildings nearby.

Decisions and opinions of the Court are born within these walls. All the arguments and hearings, all the research and discussion, the writing and giving of opinions, besides activities concerning petitions before the tribunal, take place here. The huge colonnaded edifice with its beautiful carved marble and American quartered white oak symbolizes "the national ideal of justice in the highest sphere of activity."

As one approaches the Supreme Court Building, a feeling of reverence tinged with awe inspires the beholder. Before one climbs the wide stone steps to the main entrance, a glance at the bronze flagpole bases covered with allegorical designs, at sculptured figures and marble statues, makes one stop to ponder the significance and essence of the Court. Above the sixteen gigantic marble pillars that support the roof of the handsome portico at the main entrance on the west is the gleaming façade

with the inscription "Equal Justice Under Law." Inside the
Great Hall or main corridor, one goes through huge sliding
bronze doors decorated with relief panels depicting historic
and legendary scenes, then through solid oak doors that open
into the Court Chamber, the central room of the building,
where the Court's main business is carried out.

The eastern section of the main floor houses the private
suites of the nine Justices, their robing rooms (formerly, they
donned their judicial robes as they mounted the Bench), two
large conference rooms, and the offices of the Marshal of the
Court and of the secretaries and law clerks. At the opposite end
are the Clerk of the Supreme Court and his staff. Offices for
the Reporter of Decisions and the Librarian of the Court are
located on the second floor. The entire third floor is devoted to
the library and its more than 200,000 volumes. Much admired
but seldom used are two marble and bronze stairways beginning near the side entrances to the courtroom. As the sanctuary
of justice, the permanent home of the Supreme Court of the
United States commands great respect.

A view of classic beauty, of serene quiet, and of stately
dignity is encountered when one enters the high-ceilinged
Chamber where the high Court sits. When the Court is in session, the nine Justices are seated on high-backed chairs behind
an elevated platform which holds the mahogany Judicial
Bench. The chairs vary in size and shape, for they are designed
and built in a special workshop in the basement to suit the
personal comfort of the individual Justices. The original
straight-line Bench was changed to a half-hexagon shape by
Chief Justice Warren E. Burger in 1972. This gives all nine
Justices the benefit of better sight and sound when the Court is
in session. It also permits the Chief Justice and the two senior
Associate Justices to be seated in the center section, with the
other six Justices on both sides of them, seated according to
their seniority. The Justice most recently appointed to the
Bench always sits at the extreme left of the Chief Justice. When
a Justice dies or retires and a new member is appointed, the
chair at the left end is moved to the right end, thus putting the
new appointee's chair in its proper place. However, when a new
Chief Justice ascends the Bench, he occupies the middle chair

from his first day in office. Spectators sit in the rear of the courtroom and are admitted as seats become available. The space between them and the Justices is reserved for attorneys pleading cases, for other members of the bar, and for the press. A tableau of the Ten Commandments is seen directly above the Bench, between two figures representing the Majesty of the Law and the Power of Government.

By law, the term of the Supreme Court begins on the first Monday in October; it usually concludes in late June. However, the unusually long 1973–1974 term ran until July 25, with over 5,000 cases on the Court docket for the first time in history. The term is divided among hearing cases, delivering decisions, intervening recesses, and writing opinions. Daily sessions of the Court are open to the public. The Supreme Court convenes promptly at 10 A.M. and is formally adjourned at 2:30 P.M. The Clerk and the Marshal of the Court, dressed in formal attire, sit at their desks at either end of the Bench. Those present in the courtroom arise and remain standing when, precisely at ten, the Marshal raps his gavel and announces, "The Honorable, the Chief Justice and the Associate Justices of the Supreme Court of the United States!" The nine black-robed Justices then walk to their chairs. On the Bench in front of them are briefs, papers, pencils, and pens. The Marshal of the Court then demands complete silence within the chamber by calling out three times the traditional "Oyez!"—a cry which means "Hear ye." Following this, he proclaims, "All persons having business before the Honorable, the Supreme Court of the United States, are admonished to draw near and give their attention, for the Court is now sitting. God save the United States and this Honorable Court!" As his gavel falls, the Justices and all other persons present are seated.

The Supreme Court is now in session. The first order of business is the daily custom of admitting attorneys to its bar. The first lawyers who were admitted, on February 5, 1790, included Richard Harrison of New York, Elias Boudinot of New Jersey, and Thomas Hartly of Pennsylvania. Approximately 3,000 lawyers now come to the Court each year from all parts of the nation. After the candidates are announced and introduced by the Clerk of the Court and by their sponsors, a

word of welcome is extended to them by the Chief Justice. The
Clerk of the Court then administers the oath to the new members.

Next in the order of business, formal opinions which have
been decided by the Justices in conference are delivered, generally on Mondays, although they may be announced on any
day that the Court is in session. Immediately after the presenta-
tion of opinions, orders of the Court can be discharged. The
Judicial body then divides its time between the hearing of new
cases and recesses.

Since most of the petitions involve the review of decisions
of the lower courts, a record of those courts' proceedings, with
the arguments of each side in printed briefs, is presented to the
Supreme Court. There is no jury and no witnesses are heard.
Oral argument is heard only in cases that are granted full review by the Court. When a case is argued, at least six Justices of
the Court must be present. The Chief Justice then calls for the
first case on the Court docket for oral argument.

A person may argue his own case if he chooses, but cases
before the highest Court in the nation are usually pleaded by
attorneys who are members of the bar of the Court. The counsel for the petitioner, the one responsible for having the suit
brought before the Bench on a writ of certiorari, opens the
case. The counsel for the respondent, the opposing party, is
obliged to begin and end his argument immediately thereafter,
since his adversary has the right to close the case. The Attorney
General of the United States will on occasion represent the
government when it has an interest in a specific case before the
Court, but most government-related cases are argued by the
Solicitor General or his staff. As the hearing of one case is
completed, other petitions on the docket are heard in succes-
sion, without interruption except for a half-hour lunch period.
The normal procedure is for the Bench to hear oral argument
for two weeks. During this time, the Justices meet in conference
to study all the cases heard and to write their opinions.

The Court has no public session on Fridays or Saturdays.
On Friday, the Justices hold their weekly conference in private.
Then they discuss and vote on the petitions argued and select
the cases to be considered during the next two-week Court

sitting. These conferences are conducted in absolute privacy, so that the Justices may freely discuss the cases among themselves. No clerks, stenographers, secretaries, or pages of the Court are present.

Upon entering the room, each Justice shakes hands with each of the others present. The Chief Justice opens the conference by reading the first case on the day's list and then discusses it. He then yields to the senior Associate Justice, and so on down the line until each Justice who wishes to be heard has spoken. There is no time limit. The speaker is never interrupted. After the discussion of a case has ended, the vote is taken. A docket book, which is kept locked, records the votes. A formal vote begins with the junior Justice and moves up through the ranks of seniority, with the Chief Justice voting last. In this way, the newer Justices are not influenced by their seniors. A majority opinion by the participating Justices is necessary to hand down a Court decision on a case. If he has voted with the majority, the Chief Justice assigns to an Associate Justice the task of writing the Court's opinion. If he is in dissent, the senior member of the majority makes the assignment. This often enables the Chief Justice to write decisions in important cases if he so desires.

All Court decisions are determined by the majority vote of the Justices. A new hearing may be scheduled if no decision is reached on a case. A dissenting opinion by a Justice may be issued, giving the reasons for his disagreement with the decision of the majority. Unnecessary dissent can sometimes be harmful and tends to shake public confidence in the Court's final conclusion.

A Justice who has voted with the majority may write a concurring opinion if his reasons for reaching the same conclusion differ from those expressed in the majority opinion of the Court. When the Court reconvenes, the opinions are delivered by their authors. To explain the reasons behind their decisions, the Justices put them in writing, enabling the American people to study the results. This practice also helps to keep a check on the power of the Court through public discussion and criticism.

Whoever writes the opinion usually signs it. Opinions of assent or dissent are also signed by the Justices who wrote them.

During the 1946–1947 Supreme Court term, a total of 231 dissents were cast by the Justices. Whenever the entire Court concurs in a petition, the opinion bears no signature. In writing Court opinions, the Justices consider the circumstances of the petition, the period in which the case occurred, and the language and history of the statute, as well as the intent of both the lawmakers and the architects of the Constitution.

The workings of the high Court are conducted in a similar pattern each year. Once all of the cases before it have been heard and decided, the annual term of the Supreme Court is concluded. Although the Court is adjourned for the summer until the first Monday in October, the Justices devote much of the three-month interval to the review of cases and to writing preliminary opinions about petitions to be heard during the next term. However, the Chief Justice can call a special Court session if some urgent national problem should arise. This occurred in 1942 during World War II, when a question concerning German saboteurs had to be decided. Thus the Court's role as the sole interpreter of the Constitution continues to reflect the dramatic change characteristic of each period in history.

The main work of the Supreme Court is its decisions. Opinions handed down by the Court can change not only laws, but entire social policies affecting the lives of all Americans. The third branch of government is charged with reaching decisions to break down the unjust barriers that threaten the unity of the country. America's search for justice is concluded with the Court's decisions, announced in the Court Chamber.

The workload of the Court is heavy and takes up a great deal of time. The nine Justices themselves review all of the cases and petitions that come to the Court for certiorari, even if refusal of "cert" is already assured. Usually two law clerks assist each Justice, although three are assigned to the Chief Justice, and do research on every case. These clerks are prominent law school graduates—a privileged few—who acquire an enviable legal background which helps to further their own professional careers. Changing times can influence the Justices' interpretation of current questions and problems and thereby keep our judicial system flexible and adaptable. The judicial authority granted to the Supreme Court in Article III of the Constitution ends with its decision for one side or the other.

Most of the Justices spend long, lonely hours writing Court opinions, for it is hard work. Their conclusions reflect their own personal attitudes combined with their legal beliefs. Informal debate, discussion, and voting take place during the conference only after the merits of each case have been considered. In the past a lack of harmony has often prevailed, sometimes to excess. When nine men with different backgrounds, views, and skills are assembled, it is inevitable that conflict will arise within the Court. Even health impediments, such as hearing problems, lack of normal limb movement, or lasting illness, may disrupt the business of the Court. Opinions with inaccurate wording, or the inability of one of the nine Justices to carry his fair load, can cause a loss of enthusiasm among the other members. Working in close quarters also adds to the tension. Fortunately, however, decorum is generally preserved. Argument and conflict among the Justices is rarely if ever observed by the public. Despite some private confrontations, most of the Justices maintain a mutual respect for and a friendly relationship with their peers.

Because a Supreme Court Justice possesses great knowledge of the law and high standards of conduct, he is able to preserve both an individual and an institutional outlook in his judicial pronouncements.

Groups of Justices sometimes organize themselves in "voting blocs," but never in the history of the Court has this method been used to obstruct a just decision. Any man who sits on the Bench has satisfied his one desire: to have an opportunity to put into practice his understanding of justice as the Constitution intended. Circumstances surrounding similar cases in the course of Court proceedings can alter the views of one Justice or of a group, and, consequently, dissent from an opinion may occur instead of an expected assent. In brief, the individual Justice may be opposed to the opinion of the others, but in the end each will use his own beliefs and knowledge effectively in the execution of his duty. A Justice who would use the prestige of his office for personal gain does not deserve the right to sit on the Supreme Court Bench. He can be removed through impeachment or step down from the high office of his own volition.

After days spent in thorough research and deep concentration, the Justice chosen to write the Court's opinion charts his ideas and composes a first draft. When he feels that he has an indisputable document, it goes to the print shop in the basement of the Court building, where it is printed in secret. Absolute security protects the workings of the Court. The copies are returned to the writer, and the task of revision begins. Many changes may be incorporated before the eight Associates are called upon to make comments and to discuss concepts and phraseology which they deem necessary. A Justice frequently changes his draft ten or more times before it becomes the final decision of the Supreme Court. It is then returned to the print shop, where the corrected proofs are set into a final draft. Several copies are given to the Court's press officer and to the Clerk of the Court for preservation. The findings of the Court are kept confidential until an official announcement is made simultaneously to all parties involved. Untimely declaration of some decisions could possibly disrupt the stock market and even the nation's economy.

Following the public announcement in the Court Chamber of the decision by the author of the majority opinion, the concurring and dissenting opinions are read and recognized by the Court and become part of the Court record. Reporters are handed copies in the press room as soon as a decision is announced. People from the various news media rush the decision to their co-workers by means of telephones and teletype machines. Finally, Supreme Court decisions that have taken weeks and months to become laws are released to the world at the same time that they are delivered in the courtroom. Television and radio help expedite the reporting of Court business. Thus from the white marble building of the most powerful Court in the world flows a constant stream of law to guide and protect Americanism.

Chapter III

In the
Beginning

THE SUPREME COURT OF THE UNITED STATES is an institution steeped in traditions that have developed throughout its long history. In its chambers part of the nation's body of law has been written. Its judgments and decisions are recorded on the pages of history. The Constitution dictated neither the rights and exact powers of the high Court nor the manner in which the Judiciary in its entirety should be organized. The growth of the Judicial branch of government was left to the control of the Congress and to measures introduced by the early Justices of the Supreme Court. The Supreme Court's place in American history was of the utmost importance to the new government. The Court has played a vital role in shaping United States policy and has exercised firm leadership and sound judgment in the general interest of all Americans.

In its early years, the Court helped to preserve the Union; it has continued to protect national power; it has influenced economic, political, and social trends in the later development of the country; and it has defined the principles of international law and treaties. The authors of the Constitution were acutely aware that men are subject to the evils that accompany great power. They wisely distributed authority among various parts of government and further divided the national power into three branches.

Article III of the Constitution provides that "The judicial Power of the United States, shall be vested in one supreme Court, and in such inferior Courts as the Congress may from time to time ordain and establish." It also enumerates the cases to be decided by the tribunal and the scope of its appellate jurisdiction.

The Judiciary Act of 1789, the first bill introduced in the United States Senate, provided for a Supreme Court and a Federal court system that set up Federal district courts throughout the country. It was one of the most significant and effective acts ever to be passed by the Legislative branch of the government.

The Supreme Court's power is derived from the Constitution. During its history, the Court has freely and often boldly asserted its power and jurisdiction and consequently has seldom been free from public criticism. From time to time, drastic proposals for the Court's reform and even for its end have been introduced. None have succeeded. Most Americans have maintained a conservative view of the high tribunal. Each generation has taken judicial review for granted and has accepted the process on its accumulated merits. The Court's power remains constant because the will of the people prevails.

The Supreme Court assembled for the first time in 1790—and promptly adjourned, as there was no business before it. During the first ten years of its existence, less than sixty cases came before the Court. Since state courts already existed, no petitions could be made to the high Court, as the process of taking a case to the Supreme Court or to the Court of Appeals had not yet been established. The work of the Court seemed unimportant in its early years, and some of the Justices resigned to accept more prestigious posts. The first Justices had to ride the circuits when the Court was not in session and preside as trial judges in designated districts. Because of the difficulty of travel in those times, some withdrew from their judicial appointments. The early cases before the Court were few, but the problems focused upon crucial questions of the day. The

Court docket involved petitions concerning debts with England, defining the types of cases to be heard before the Federal courts, and establishing precedents of court procedures for the American court system for all time. The shipping industry became a principal issue, which helped shape one of the Court's later roles as arbiter of international law. Most of the work of the early Court was relatively trivial and could have been decided by lower courts. However, occasional matters of national concern already justified the existence of the Supreme Court.

After fifty years, vital changes in the business of the Court occurred. In 1875, the country expanded its boundaries and increased both in population and in commerce. The Court docket involved such problems as property, insurance, and bank drafts. It also decided cases dealing with commerce, the right to trial by jury, the rights of blacks, and the right to utilize private land for public purposes and needs. The Supreme Court now heard more cases in one year than it had in the first ten years of its existence. As a result of the increased workload, the Court was unable to keep up with its business. Judiciary reforms in 1900 established new Federal appeals courts, dividing the country into circuits and creating a regional supreme court for each. This outlet reduced the overcrowded Court docket and kept the business of the Court current well into the twentieth century.

Prior to 1900, over six hundred cases a year appeared on the docket. After these Court changes, the number was reduced within a two-year period to less than three hundred. The Supreme Court was also freed from the task of handling cases for the District of Columbia. By 1925 the Court again had a tremendous backlog of cases, and it took almost two years to decide a case. As a result, the Judges' Bill, initiated by Chief Justice William Howard Taft for the purpose of granting the Court expanded power of decision within certain bounds, was put into effect to determine what cases it would hear. The high tribunal has continued to work under this declaration to the present day. Most of the cases are presented by writ of certiorari and by appeal. The Court has set down rules for accepting or denying petitions. It can use its power to confirm or overturn lower court decisions; it can hand down an opinion without hearing voice argument or reading briefs. Today, the Court's control over what cases it will decide is accepted almost without question. With a smaller docket of cases to be heard, the present Court is free to be quick and definite in its decisions.

The first Court had six members—one Chief Justice and five Associate Justices. The exact number is set by the Congress and has changed six times over the years. In 1866, the Court had seven Justices. Since 1869, it has consisted of nine members, one Chief Justice and eight Associate Justices. The official title of the head of the Court has changed over the years from Chief Justice of the United States to Chief Justice of the Supreme Court of the United States. The real distinction of the Chief Justice is that he is the head of the Judiciary branch of the Federal government; therefore, as far as official rank goes, the President and the Speaker of the House are his equals, but nobody is his superior.

The Chief Justice is the leader of the high tribunal, but this does not mean that he rules it, nor does it imply that the Associate Justices are subordinate to him. It simply indicates that he is first among equals. His duties are the same as those of his eight Associates, and his vote carries no more weight than that of a junior Justice. However, the Chief Justiceship presents an opportunity for leadership and entails certain privileges. He walks in front when the Court parades in procession; he administers the oath when a new President is inaugurated; and he presides at the trial when a President is impeached. He presides at both public and private sessions of the Court, assigns the task of writing most Court opinions to the Associate Justices, and officiates at conferences held for the judges of the lower courts. The personality and competence of the Chief Justices have been known to influence other members of the Court, and periods of the Court's history have been named after them, for example, the Marshall Court, the Warren Court, and the Burger Court.

Certainly, the Supreme Court is the smallest branch in terms of manpower, and it is the least dangerous since it has no power to enforce its own resolutions.

To be appointed to the Supreme Court is the highest distinction to which an American lawyer can aspire, yet there are no specific qualifications for this eminent position. Members of the Supreme Court are appointed by the President, subject to the advice of and confirmation by the Senate. The President of the United States may appoint anyone he chooses. His nominee does not even have to be a lawyer, or, in fact, a man. The President could choose a woman, although so far a woman has never been appointed.

An appointee is generally a prominent man who has gained a reputation for honesty, knowledge, and wisdom through many years of experience, and consequently, appointees are usually middle-aged and often elderly. Because they possess courage, integrity, and high morals, they have seldom cast a shadow of disgrace upon the Court. Most have been thoughtful men who knew the law, studied the law, and respected the law. Members of the Court past and present have been eminent members of the legal profession. Judges, attorneys, professors of law, and distinguished government officials have sat on the Bench. A Justice of the Supreme Court is the custodian of an exalted position filled with complicated obligations and fragile trusts, demanding traits so diverse that no individual aware of his own human weakness can attempt to undertake it without a severe assessment of his abilities. The duties, both mental and physical, of the early Court Justices, along with the lack of prestige attached to a Justiceship, discouraged most men from seeking and accepting a Court appointment. Today, it is one of the most desired public offices in the nation.

Since the first decade of the Court's existence, all but three Presidents—William Henry Harrison, Zachary Taylor, and Andrew Johnson—have named Justices to the Supreme Court. Every President who has served one full term in office has nominated at least one Justice. George Washington holds the record, with eleven nominations, including three Chief Justices. Franklin D. Roosevelt is next, with nine appointments. He also elevated Harlan Fiske Stone from Associate Justice to Chief Justice during his Presidency. William Howard Taft, who later became Chief Justice, named six Justices to the high Court.

Through the years, only eleven Supreme Court nominees have been rejected by the Senate. A few nominations have been recalled, delayed, or not acted upon. Although John Rutledge served four months as Chief Justice in 1795, he was denied the lifetime position because the Senate failed to confirm his appointment. In 1969 and 1970 President Richard M. Nixon's appointees, Clement F. Haynsworth, Jr., of South Carolina and G. Harrold Carswell of Florida, became the first nominees to be rejected by the Senate since 1930. Haynsworth's nomination was withdrawn because of doubts in the Senate about the propriety of certain of his stockholdings. Senate confirmation of Carswell, who had served for twelve years on the Federal bench, was denied because of the belief that he was a mediocre judge and because of a widespread rumor that he was a racist. These nominees were replaced with two conservative candidates, Lewis F. Powell, Jr., a Virginia lawyer and a Democrat, and William H. Rehnquist, an Assistant Attorney General and a Republican. Both were appointed by President Nixon in 1972, and their confirmation by the Senate provided the Supreme Court with its strongest conservative majority since the 1930s.

There have been fifteen Chief Justices and eighty-nine Associate Justices in the Supreme Court's long history. There have been a hundred Justices in all, since four of the Chief Justices were former Associate Justices. All members of the Supreme Court are appointed for life, or, as the Constitution puts it, "during good Behavior." The average length of service on the Bench is fifteen years. At the age of seventy, a Justice may retire with full salary if he has served ten or more years, and if he has fifteen years' tenure, he may retire from office at sixty-five and continue to receive his full salary for the remainder of his life. The present Chief Justice receives a yearly salary of $75,000; each Associate Justice receives $66,000. The salaries have varied over the years with the Chief Justice receiving relatively little more than the other members of the Court. Justices' salaries may not be reduced while they are in office. These provisions protect the Justices from political control and have helped to guarantee an independent Judiciary.

In 1957, for the first time in the history of the Court, all nine Justices held law degrees. Since that time, every member of the Supreme Court has had either the LL.B. (Bachelor of Laws) or the J.D. (Doctor of Law) degree, its more recent equivalent. Few Justices have voluntarily left the Bench while they were still capable of judicial service. Some have created problems by refusing to resign after their judicial capacities had failed. However, several have left the prestigious post to accept other important positions or careers; others have stepped down to enjoy the peace of retirement.

Chapter IV

The Chief Justices

THE BACKGROUND OF EACH CHIEF JUSTICE, as well as the decisions handed down during his term on the Bench, has played a vital role in the history of the Court. The office of Chief Justice of the United States was created on September 24, 1789, by the Judiciary Bill, which also approved the appointment of five Associate Justices. Two days later, John Jay became the first Chief Justice (1789–1795) of the highest Court in the nation. He was nominated by President George Washington, and his appointment was immediately confirmed by the Senate.

President Washington was impressed with the outstanding abilities and distinguished service of John Jay and offered him any post he desired. There was no public office Jay preferred to that of Chief Justice. The character of his mind, his familiarity with the principles underlying American institutions, and especially his experience as head of the highest court of New York State fitted him for the position.

Justice Jay was extremely prudent, discreet, and shrewd, and though he was devoted to the truth, he refrained from saying more than was necessary. He always pursued the course that his intelligence and judgment recommended, regardless of creed or party, even in religious matters. In politics, Jay preserved his independence of action, never losing the courage to make unpopular decisions. His quick mind and diplomatic skill were of great value to the early leaders of the new government. John Jay was a great defender of freedom. Prior to his appointment as Chief Justice, Jay had served as President of the Continental Congress, as Minister to Spain, and had helped to organize the Treaty of Paris in 1783. He had become the Secretary of Foreign Affairs in 1784. Jay was the author of the New York State Constitution, which later provided a model for parts of the United States Constitution.

John Jay was forty-four years old when he became Chief Justice. Someone who knew him remarked, "When the ermine of the judicial robe fell on John Jay, it touched nothing less spotless than itself." In his letter of appointment, George Washington voiced his personal satisfaction at greeting Jay as the leader of "that department which must be considered as the keystone of our political fabric."

On February 1, 1790, the Supreme Court met for the first time in the Royal Exchange Building in New York City, which was the nation's capital at that time. When the capital was moved to Philadelphia, the Court was first housed in Independence Hall and later in the City Hall. In 1800, when Washington, D.C., became the nation's permanent capital, the high tribunal met in the Capitol Building and in private homes. In 1860 the Court assembled in a few rooms of the Senate Chambers, remaining there for seventy-five years. Since 1935 the Judiciary has convened in its own building, designed by Architect Cass Gilbert as "a building of dignity and importance suitable for its use as the permanent home of the Supreme Court of the United States."

On February 1, 1790, Chief Justice John Jay and two Associate Justices, James Wilson (1789–1798), a signer of the Constitution from Pennsylvania, and William Cushing (1790–1810), a noted jurist from Massachusetts and the oldest member of the new Court, met for the first assembly of the Supreme Court of the United States. The problems of travel delayed the arrival of the majority of the Justices by a day, and the Chief Justice postponed the first formal meeting of the high Court until February 2. The other Justices included John Rutledge (1790–1791), a former governor and Chief Justice of the Supreme Court of South Carolina; John Blair (1790–1796), a past Chief Justice of Virginia's Court of Appeals; and thirty-eight-year-old James Iredell (1790–1799), the youngest member of the early Court and a former attorney general of North Carolina. Iredell replaced Robert Hanson Harrison, who had resigned the Justiceship only five days after his confirmation by the Senate in order to become chancellor of the State of Maryland.

All of the original Justices belonged to the Federalist party. Chief Justice Jay and his colleagues were dressed in robes trimmed in gold and scarlet, similar to the traditional gown worn by British judges. However, the solemn-looking wig was discarded after Justice Cushing was met with laughter and cheers as he came in wearing a white wig. Since no business required immediate attention, the Court was adjourned.

The early sessions of the Court were occupied with the adoption of rules governing the administration and function of Court proceedings. A Clerk of the Court was selected, and attorneys were admitted to practice before the Bench. At that time, members of the bar appeared in Court dressed in formal "morning clothes." Today, a lawyer usually approaches the Bench wearing a dark business suit and a necktie. However, members of the Department of Justice and other attorneys representing the United States government still follow the tradition of formal dress. Because of the lack of cases, the Court adjourned for six months. During its second year, the first petitions reached the Supreme Court. The first formal decisions were handed down by the Justices in 1792, the third year of the Court's existence.

Twice a year, when the Supreme Court was not in session, the Justices had to ride the circuit and conduct other court business in the districts assigned to them. These were divided into the Middle, the Eastern, and the Southern circuits. The people became acquainted with the principles of the Supreme Court through their contact with the circuit court judges.

All the Justices, and especially the Chief Justice, are in a position of great judicial power when they are sitting on the Bench. Their decisions reflect not only their legal knowledges, but also their personal beliefs, concepts, and attitudes; therefore, any comprehension of the high Court demands an understanding of the men inside the robes. Since the Chief Justice often sets the tone for the Court, an insight into his background and character is essential to an understanding of the Supreme Court. All these men must be good and honest in order to fulfill their role as arbiters of the law.

Despite the many changes during its history, the Supreme Court has remained basically the same institution since its inauguration in 1790. It has maintained many customs of the past, such as the use of quill pens and the "conference handshake" at the beginning of each conference meeting. This precedent was established in the late nineteenth century during the Justiceship of Melville W. Fuller (1888–1910). The early decisions have also had lasting influence on the deliberations of the Supreme Court down to the present day.

During John Jay's short term on the Bench, three major doctrines of the Supreme Court were established. The Court became independent and no longer subject to control by the other branches of government. The Court's jurisdiction was gradually found to be over that of the state governments. Thus the first Chief Justice established beyond doubt the role of the Supreme Court as the interpreter of the Constitution. It was John Jay, also, who had great influence in shaping the United States foreign policy.

When John Jay took his seat on the Bench, he realized that the successful operation of the country's new independent government would depend largely upon his interpretation of its powers, with his belief in justice and good faith to guide him. The most important case to come before the Court during Jay's tenure was an action begun in 1792 by a private citizen against the state. It involved the question of whether an individual could sue a sovereign state in the Federal courts. The Chief Justice pointed out that a state had the power to sue a private citizen; therefore, why could not a man do the same to the state, which was simply a body of his fellow citizens? The Constitution enabled a state to be a plaintiff, but said nothing about its being a defendant in a suit brought by an individual. Jay considered the process of recourse to the courts' decision to be wise, honest, and useful. It thus became a basic point of law that the lowliest citizen could not be denied the means of obtaining justice, whether from one other citizen or from millions. During his four years as Chief Justice, John Jay contributed to the growth of confidence in and respect for the Court by his honesty and faultless conduct. He helped maintain the doctrine of the separation of powers, since he firmly believed that this was the essence of good government. He wished to keep the Court free of political complications in the same way that he hoped his Associates would keep themselves free from anything which might bias their judgment.

When John Jay resigned as Chief Justice to become governor of New York in 1795, President Washington readily accepted Associate Justice John Rutledge's request for the post. A noted statesman and jurist, Rutledge became the second Chief Justice of the Court on August 12, 1795, at the age of fifty-five. He was also the only Chief Justice later to vacate the office because of Senate rejection. Fifteen men have served the Supreme Court as Chief Justice. All but Rutledge were confirmed by the Senate. His political tactics concerning the Jay Treaty, negotiated in 1794 to end the disputes between the United States and Great Britain stemming from the Revolutionary War, along with gossip about his mental ability, ended his career as the head of the Judiciary. He served only one term, during August, and his name appears on two opinions handed down during the session. His Chief Justiceship ended on December 15, 1795, when the Senate reconvened and promptly rejected his appointment.

After William Cushing, the senior Associate Justice from Massachusetts, had declined to fill the vacancy, the President appointed Oliver Ellsworth as the third Chief Justice (1796–1800) of the Supreme Court on March 4, 1796. This famed lawyer and jurist from Connecticut took the judicial oath four days later. A brilliant scholar, Ellsworth had served in the Continental Congress and had been a delegate to the Constitutional Convention of 1787. The recognition he gained as a leader of the Connecticut bar provided him with a thriving practice. His legal background included service as a state's attorney and a judge of the superior court of his native state. He was the first United States Senator from Connecticut, a post he held from 1789 to 1795. He helped to draft the United States Constitution, but his signature does not appear on the famous document, since he was not present when the Convention adjourned. He was considered the principal author of the Judiciary Bill. His cherished dream was to have the bill enacted; he was its constant promoter, defender, and interpreter on the floor of the Senate. He wished to see a completely independent system of state courts. While still a Senator, Ellsworth had the satisfaction of seeing the Judiciary Bill passed. Much of this bill, which established the structure of the Federal courts, is still in effect today.

For almost four years, Chief Justice Ellsworth was busily occupied with the duties of his office, which at that time included the difficult task of riding the Federal circuit. The shortness of his term as Chief Justice and the fact that he was immediately followed in office by the great John Marshall are two reasons he does not rank higher in fame among the Chief Justices. Ellsworth's decisions, while few and short, are marked by sound common sense, without profound legal background. He was primarily a staunch defender of any cause he felt was right. A politician as well as a statesman, he was not above using party politics to accomplish his goals. This political talent, which undoubtedly contributed much to his success at the bar and to his work both in the Congress and Senate, was less of a help to him in judicial matters, and he resigned from the Court in 1800.

Before he was succeeded in the White House by Thomas Jefferson, President John Adams appointed John Marshall, then his Secretary of State, as the fourth Chief Justice (1801–1835). John Marshall was nominated on January 20, 1801. The Senate confirmed his appointment to the Chief Justiceship seven days later. His nomination was not welcomed in all quarters. On February 4, 1801, John Marshall, with his customary lack of speed, accepted and took his seat on the Judicial Bench, thereby opening Court for the first time in Washington, D.C., the new capital on the Potomac. Marshall's appointment was to have a significant and lasting effect on the Court. In the pages of history, he would become known as "the man who made the Supreme Court." When John Jay resigned in 1795, he remarked that the Court could never achieve its rightful authority. Less than forty years later, John Marshall said that he would rather be Chief Justice than President. No other American did so much as he to establish American judicial power and to put into practice the true meaning of the Constitution. In his thirty-four years as Chief Justice, the decisions of the Supreme Court were sometimes bitterly criticized, but today his interpretations of the law are almost universally accepted. His decisions in various areas of the law set up precedents which have guided the Court for years.

Marshall believed that only a strong Federal government could enable the United States to act effectively as a nation; his decisions helped make this theory a reality. Above all, he set standards for a broad translation of the implied powers of the Federal government and of the commerce clause in the Constitution. He upheld the power of the Congress to create the United States Bank, thus firmly establishing the principle that in case of conflict Federal power must prevail over state power. His definition of the National Power over interstate commerce set regulations which are still in force today.

Marshall became Chief Justice at a time when the present-day cooperation among the three branches of government had not yet been established, nor was the relationship between the national government and the states clear. It fell to Marshall to solve these problems. He believed in both nationalism and individualism. His forcefulness in interpreting the Constitution became most apparent after 1811. From that time until his death in 1835, most of the Justices who sat on the Bench were appointed by Presidents who strongly opposed Marshall's policies. The new Justices also challenged him, but almost invariably they soon found themselves in agreement with his opinions. For these reasons John Marshall has been called the "Second Father of the Constitution" and has been regarded as the greatest jurist in American history. His fame as Chief Justice has overshadowed his numerous other services to the nation. He always placed emphasis on the importance of the Constitution, the supremacy of Federal law, and the need for payment of debts. Marshall always won his point, even when defeat seemed certain. He used his daily Court practice to educate himself in the law. He quoted few authorities in his judicial opinions, in striking contrast to most judges.

The Supreme Court had not yet won public respect when Marshall took office, so that it was difficult to find qualified men to serve as Associate Justices. Many felt that the Court would never have much influence on the major questions and problems of the day. But thirty-four years later, when Chief Justice Marshall died on July 6, 1835, the Supreme Court had become a vigorous and effective branch of the government, deeply rooted for all time through his decisions. Marshall strongly believed that the Supreme Court was the final arbiter of the law and that the Court was to speak through its Chief Justice. He upheld the right of the United States government to enforce the laws of the nation, even against the individual states, if state laws conflicted with the Constitution or Federal statutes. His contributions to the Court were many: he established judicial review, made the Court one of the major political powers of the nation, and infused an ancient legal tradition with new meaning. In 1803 the first Court decision which ruled a Federal law unconstitutional (*Marbury v. Madison*) was handed down. A fighting Chief Justice, he established the right of the Court to define its original jurisdiction as prescribed by the Constitution, asserting that Congress could not change it by law.

The fifth Chief Justice of the United States Supreme Court was Roger Brooke Taney (1836–1864). President Andrew Jackson nominated him for the office upon the death of John Marshall. His appointment was confirmed by the Senate after strong opposition, and the judicial oath was administered to him on March 28, 1836. He was then fifty-nine. His Chief Justiceship was to last for twenty-eight years. This great jurist continued his predecessor's interpretation of the Constitution. He also stressed the power of the Supreme Court to determine the constitutionality of both national and state law. His early legal and political training provided the background for his career as an esteemed member of the bar.

Before joining the Democratic party, Roger Taney had been a leader of the Federalist Party during its last few years of existence. He had served in the state senate of Maryland and in the Treasury Department, where he was a strong opponent of the Bank of the United States. When the Senate majority changed in 1836, he was confirmed as Chief Justice of the Supreme Court, although his nomination as Associate Justice had been rejected just a year earlier. Taney's interest in the rights of Negroes, whether free or slave, drew severe criticism because of his aristocratic background. His reluctant decision on the slavery issue in the famous Dred Scott case of 1857 denied citizenship to all Negroes and prevented the Congress from prohibiting slavery in the nation's new territories. Taney declared that slaves were property and that the rights of their owners would be violated if the Congress were allowed to abolish slavery in the new states. His was cited as the majority opinion, since each Associate Justice had written a separate opinion. The Dred Scott decision also influenced the adoption of the Fourteenth Amendment to the Constitution in 1868, which granted citizenship and civil rights to former slaves. It was the belief of many that the author of the Dred Scott decision not only had degraded the efficiency of the Court, but had helped provoke the Civil War. With the passage of time, resentment toward him has faded, and his character and motives have become more fully understood. During his term, the Court adjusted to a changing America, and Roger Taney combined tradition with flexibility in order to maintain and develop judicial supremacy.

Despite personal doubts and dislikes, President Abraham Lincoln chose to nominate his former Secretary of the Treasury, Salmon Portland Chase (1864–1873), to succeed Taney as Chief Justice. Most of Chase's years as head of the Judiciary fell during the violent Reconstruction period of American history. A distinguished Secretary of the Treasury during the Civil War, he had resigned his post because of a policy dispute with Lincoln. He has been credited with the organization of our present national banking system. As Chief Justice, Chase administered the Presidential oath to Andrew Johnson and later presided over his impeachment trial. He served as head of the high tribunal for eight years after taking the oath on December 15, 1864. His opinions as Chief Justice are noted for a practical emphasis on major doctrines rather than for their legal acumen.

Chase had served as United States Senator from Ohio and was determined to write into national law, wherever possible, a policy of slavery limitation. Despite expressions of contempt from the opposition, Chase publicly defended fugitive slaves, and was called the "Attorney General for runaway Negroes." In the altered political horizon created by the downfall of the Whigs and the rise of the Republican party, Salmon Chase joined the Republicans. He was elected to serve two terms as governor of Ohio but was twice denied the Presidential nomination of his party. His overweening ambition for the Presidency was thwarted in 1868, when the Republicans refused him the nomination. When he sensed a political rebirth in that party, Chase described himself as an independent Democrat. However, he once again failed to be nominated.

The Supreme Court over which he presided was faced by a hostile Congress and was subjected to unusual burdens in a series of complex cases. In 1870, Chase delivered the opinion for the Court declaring unconstitutional that part of the Legal Tender Act of 1862 which had made the "greenbacks"—paper money, as opposed to gold or silver—legal payment for existing contracts at the time the bill was passed. As Treasury Secretary, Chase himself had issued these government notes, and now he was severely attacked for making them illegal. Although his years as Chief Justice witnessed the realization of his cherished hope for the abolition of slavery and the restoration of the Union, he experienced personal abuse, disappointment, and great loss of dignity, because of his handling of postwar problems and corruption. Salmon Portland Chase was probably the least happy of our Chief Justices.

Morrison Remick Waite, one of the founders of the Republican party, had a definite impact on his profession early in his career. He climbed the ladder of legal success, handling numerous cases pertaining to finance, such as mortgages, titles, and monetary adjustments. He became a recognized authority on the law of real estate and legal titles. It was this training which was later to make him indispensable to the interests of the railroads. He was born in Lyme, Connecticut, was graduated from Yale College, and was admitted to the bar in 1839. Most of his law practice was in Ohio. Waite had a lifetime interest in civic affairs and took an active part in the election of William Henry Harrison to the Presidency. He served in the Ohio state legislature but was twice defeated as a candidate for the Congress. He also promoted the cause of the Union during the Civil War and later served with the American counsel in the Geneva Arbitration on the *Alabama* claims.

Ulysses S. Grant, the eighteenth President of the United States, nominated him to the Bench, and on March 4, 1874, Morrison Remick Waite was installed as the seventh Chief Justice (1874–1888) of the Supreme Court. Although he had no previous experience as a judge and had never pleaded a case before the Court over which he was to preside, Morrison Waite received unanimous Senate confirmation.

During his tenure, the Court was to decide more than a thousand cases. The power of state governments to regulate business was one of the major decisions he handed down. The farmers of the Midwest had appealed to the state governments to fix uniform railroad and warehouse rates. These appeals became known as the Granger cases. Waite upheld the state laws, against the farmers. The petition of *Munn v. Illinois* was the most significant of these cases.

In a limitation on state power, Waite initiated the first steps toward the modern interpretation of due-process-of-law ruling. This made the Supreme Court the final judge in all legal controversy and was a major contribution to the law. Although a defender of states' rights, he increased Congressional control over interstate commerce by ruling that the government could regulate private property in the public interest. In his later years as Chief Justice, Waite refused to be considered as a Presidential candidate, since he believed it wrong to use the Supreme Court Bench as a steppingstone to political office.

Melville Weston Fuller (1888–1910) succeeded Morrison Waite as Chief Justice and served in that capacity for twenty-one years. His nomination to the Court, however, had met with difficulties. Fuller was a staunch Democrat; his nomination was confirmed by a largely Republican Senate only after a prolonged delayed vote. The opposition was largely partisan, caused in part by his lukewarm loyalty to the Union during the Civil War. Because of his personal and legal abilities, Fuller became known as the business manager of the Court. He was a capable Court administrator, and he performed his judicial duties with a versatility that demonstrated his extraordinary intelligence and displayed the depth of his training before the Court.

His early career had set him apart as a strong contender for high legal office. Fuller's knowledge of canon law made him an asset to the bar. His cases also involved contract monopoly among gas companies in Chicago and long-term franchises held by street railways in that city. When he was appointed to the Supreme Court, he had already won the complete confidence of Bench and bar. Prior to his Chief Justiceship, Fuller had declined two diplomatic posts offered him by President Grover Cleveland. Although born in Augusta, Maine, he always called Chicago the home of his heart. It was there that Fuller worked as a corporation lawyer, became a member of the Illinois legislature and a delegate to the Democratic national conventions, and was a frequent orator for the city's bar association.

Fuller undertook his Court duties during a period of unsurpassed industrial growth, when established national traditions were breaking up, and the struggle between capital and labor was mounting. The Chief Justice applied constitutional restraints to curb the conflict. He supported the doctrine of states' rights and was a sincere believer in individualism. He also believed in limitations on Congressional power. His numerous legal decisions are marked by directness, clarity of reasoning, and common sense. Melville Fuller handed down two well-known decisions which declared the national income tax unconstitutional and greatly weakened the Sherman Anti-Trust Act of 1890. Probably no successor has equaled him as a business manager of the Court, or enjoyed the admiration of his colleagues and of the bar to such a degree.

The ninth Chief Justice (1910–1921), Edward Douglass White, was nominated by President William Howard Taft and took the oath of office on December 19, 1910. His career had already included election to the Louisiana Senate and appointment to the state supreme court. He had been a member of the United States Senate and had been appointed an Associate Justice in 1894 by President Grover Cleveland. He served as Associate Justice for sixteen years before his appointment as Chief Justice. White was the first Associate Justice to be appointed to the Chief Justiceship. President Taft was most likely influenced by his desire to politically break the "Solid South." White, who came from Louisiana, was the second Democrat and Catholic to preside over the U.S. Supreme Court. (Roger B. Taney was the other.)

Over seven hundred opinions were handed down by White during his tenure. He had a phenomenal memory; he apparently knew his decisions by heart, including volume and page citations, and seldom referred to the text. He was a capable presiding Justice whose work in the Court was done with remarkable energy and speed. He did much to reach compromises in order to reconcile differences of opinion among the members of the Court.

Earlier, prior to his Chief Justiceship, a few decisions of the high Court had caused widespread criticism of the Court. Agitation for a restraint upon judicial review reached its peak shortly after White took command. It is difficult to generalize about the decisions the White Court handed down. He was a middle-of-the-road man. Probably the most important decision he ever wrote was when, joining the liberals of the Court, he upheld the fixed minimum wage for railroad workers set down in the Adamson Act of 1916. He supported the right of the Federal government to issue injunctions in labor disputes. The Chief Justice practiced the rule of reason in his antitrust decisions demanding that the monopolies of the Standard Oil Company and the American Tobacco Company be broken up. At the time of his death in 1921, someone remarked that his judicial opinions were not models to be followed by others. There was little clarity in his reasoning, and his opinions were usually long and involved. However, Edward White possessed both dignity and humility, and was well-liked, especially among young and inexperienced attorneys who appeared before his Court.

William Howard Taft's lifelong desire to sit on the Supreme Court Bench was not realized until late in his career. His early years were spent in law practice and in service in Manila; then came his traumatic Presidency, and finally his elevation to the Bench. Taft is the only man in U.S. history to serve first as President, then as Chief Justice. He had never wished to be President. His greatest hope was to be a Justice of the Supreme Court. As a judge, he had little fondness for politics. Except for the Presidency, Taft was elected to only one other public office by popular vote, and that was a five-year term on the Ohio supreme court.

William Howard Taft received appointments from three Presidents. Under William McKinley, he served as the first civil governor of the Philippine Islands. Theodore Roosevelt appointed him to his cabinet as Secretary of War. After his term as President (1909–1913), he became professor of constitutional law at Yale University and was elected president of the American Bar Association. In 1921, Warren G. Harding nominated Taft as the tenth Chief Justice (1921–1930) of the Supreme Court. He took the judicial oath on July 11, 1921, at the age of sixty-three.

After eight years, he left his post because of ill health. He regarded his Chief Justiceship as the greatest honor of his life. Always cautious in his use of power in the White House, as head of the Judiciary he went to unprecedented lengths for judicial reform. At that time the Court docket was overloaded with litigation, much of it of minor importance. Urged by his persuasive arguments, the Congress passed the Judges' Act in 1925, which gave the Supreme Court greater powers of discretion in choosing the cases to be heard.

Taft also established a conference for circuit court judges and used his influence to get the Supreme Court its own building. His reform of judicial administration and procedure greatly increased the efficiency of the courts, in which result he took personal pride. He believed that fair and effective courts could eliminate social unrest and check the demand for radical social change. Above all, he viewed the Supreme Court as the guardian of the Constitution and of property rights. He became more conservative as he grew older, opposing such liberal colleagues as Oliver Wendell Holmes, Louis D. Brandeis, and Harlan F. Stone. It was during his later years that the phrase "Holmes, Brandeis, and Stone dissent" became popular. Even though these dissents displeased him, the years Taft spent as Chief Justice were extremely happy ones. He had done more than his share of the Court's heavy workload and had often served as adviser to President Calvin Coolidge. A month after his retirement from the Bench, Chief Justice William Howard Taft died. He was the first President to be buried in Arlington National Cemetery in Virginia. John F. Kennedy was the second, in 1963.

Charles Evans Hughes of New York became Chief Justice (1930–1941) of the Supreme Court during a time when controversy occupied the Court. A defender of human liberties, Hughes gained recognition through his unstinting service to his country. His professional career was a distinguished one. He served as a judge of the World Court, as Secretary of State under Presidents Harding and Coolidge, and as governor of New York. He was also appointed Associate Justice (1910–1916) by William Howard Taft, and he was a Republican candidate for the Presidency. International affairs also occupied part of his career. He had a successful law practice, and was in demand as a corporation lawyer. As a member of the New York legislature, Hughes investigated the gas and insurance companies and was widely acclaimed as the man who changed the insurance business "from a public swindle into a public trust." Powerful businessmen squirmed under his stern interrogation as he proceeded to demonstrate that links existed between corrupt politics and corrupt finance. Newspapers called him a wizard of the bar.

Although Charles Evans Hughes has often been referred to as the greatest Chief Justice since John Marshall, his appointment by President Herbert Hoover met with Senate opposition and objections by those who believed that his public life was influenced by strong political contact with the world of finance. Following his confirmation, he took the judicial oath on February 24, 1930, and served as Chief Justice for eleven years. After he had sat only one year on the Bench, the President, Senators, and Hughes's colleagues were either pleased or annoyed to find that he had joined the Court's liberals in his opinions. He upheld the rights of the railway clerks to form their own labor union, and he sustained a New Jersey act regulating insurance rates. In fact, until the New Deal years, Hughes was always considered a liberal. Later no one was certain where he stood. With the liberals, Chief Justice Hughes wrote the opinions upholding the constitutionality of municipal bankruptcy acts and upholding the government in the gold cases. He extended the rights of Negroes, ruling that they had the same privileges of railroad travel as the whites.

As Chief Justice, Hughes supported the National Labor Relations Act, the Social Security laws, and the Federal Wages and Hours Act. To protect the investing public, he dissented against the power of the Securities and Exchange Commission; he also declared the Guffey Coal Act unconstitutional. He ruled against several New Deal actions, such as Franklin D. Roosevelt's court-packing plan and the National Industrial Recovery Act, leading the President to refer to the Hughes Court as "nine old men."

Under Hughes's leadership, Court sessions moved briskly. He kept a rigid schedule in order to keep the business of the Court up-to-date, and he took the time to write his own opinions, working in a room cluttered with papers. His Court decisions during a regular eight-month term were numerous. Critics argue about his opinions and about the man who wrote them. The Court of Chief Justice Hughes is marked in history as one of crisis and confusion.

The appointment of Harlan Fiske Stone as Chief Justice (1941–1946) by President Franklin D. Roosevelt met with unanimous approval by the Senate. The twelfth Chief Justice, a Republican from New York, was sworn into office on July 3, 1941, at the age of sixty-eight. His legal career, his experience and record, and his character proved him to be the right choice for the Chief Justiceship. His years on the Bench as an Associate Justice (1925–1941), as well as the skills and knowledge acquired as Attorney General and as head of the Federal Bureau of Criminal Investigation under J. Edgar Hoover, had prepared Harlan Stone for the awesome duties that now confronted him.

Chief Justice Stone worked slowly, conscious of the need for fairness and exactness. Eventually he supported the rather broad view that the Constitution could be interpreted to reflect the needs of the times. Although a conservative, he was influenced by two of his formerly liberal Associate Justices, Oliver Wendell Holmes and Louis D. Brandeis, and often voted in the Court against his own party. He believed that the Court must rule on the constitutionality rather than on the wisdom of the law.

His many years on the Supreme Court Bench were marked by three distinct areas of constitutional debate. The first involved the power of a state to bring about changes in its economic or legal order by controls, prohibitions, or taxes. A second involved debate over the authority of the United States government to originate changes in its doctrines of economy or in its established statutes. The third and final area was the great controversy over the right of the majority to control matters of conscience and expression. Stone's views, as expressed in his Supreme Court decisions, were that laws were made for human needs and that those laws must control and protect these needs, and that with reasonable compromise with the past, essential economic and social changes could be instituted for the future. It was this philosophy that led the Chief Justice to uphold in the 1940s much of the New Deal legislation of the 1930s and even to crack down especially hard on former Wall Street associates.

Stone's duties as head of the Supreme Court were many and varied. He administered the Presidential oath to Harry S Truman; he presided over cases dealing with martial law, treason, and military courts during World War II, many of which involved constitutional matters brought before the Supreme Court for the first time. It was the aim of the Chief Justice to support individual freedom and to protect human rights, especially during the difficult war years. The twelfth Chief Justice wrote hundreds of Court opinions and dissents on every aspect of the law during his years on the Bench. His opinions, phrased with caution, were often quoted in cases before his own Court. A decision on the question of whether refusal to carry arms because of religious belief was a block to U.S. citizenship (*Girouard v. United States*) illustrated his readiness to yield to legislation and to change his mind when he felt it was the right thing to do. Two opinions by Stone concerning the same question bore different outcomes.

More a politician than a judge, statesman or jurist, Frederick Moore Vinson became the thirteenth Chief Justice (1946–1953) on June 24, 1946, appointed by President Harry S Truman, whom he had served as Secretary of the Treasury. He had played a vital role in resolving financial problems and settlements at the end of World War II, and was often referred to as the economic czar of the United States. He was a Democrat from Kentucky. Vinson's legal practice entailed political duties that were the source of his great respect for the Executive branch of government. As a former Congressman and Federal judge, Vinson worked with his peers as a team, rather than as a single performer with a chorus. He lacked an appreciation of the Court as an institution. His deep personal interest in politics and his interpretation of national authority often led him to rule for the government as against the individual. He was an intelligent man, but not by habit a patient one. He studied legislation with precision and was a tenacious fighter in any debate.

Vinson was not a prominent figure early in his career, but later earned recognition for his opposition to the sales and tobacco tax. He is best remembered for his part in creating a sound tax structure through compromise with the New Deal Revenue Bill. Prior to his appointment to the Supreme Court, Vinson served with distinction as director of the Office of Economic Stabilization and the Office of War Mobilization. Perhaps his best-known decisions as Chief Justice were those upholding the rights of minority groups under the equal protection clause of the Fourteenth Amendment and his opposition to the majority opinion which held invalid President Truman's seizure of the steel companies in 1952. There are many who do not admire his contributions to American law, but hardly anyone will deny that Chief Justice Vinson was a man of great political and executive talent, an architect of legal compromise.

Earl Warren, who rose through California Republican politics to dominate the Supreme Court era that bears his name, took the judicial oath on October 4, 1953, at the age of sixty-two. At first, his appointment by Dwight D. Eisenhower drew wide criticism because of Warren's lack of private legal practice in the years preceding his Chief Justiceship. Warren soon responded by exhibiting his rigorously strict legal knowledge on such critical issues as civil rights and the economic problems that were to occupy so much of his Court's time (1953–1969).

A prominent political figure in America, Earl Warren was neither a genius nor a saint. As skilled craftsman in the field of democratic government, he expressed himself openly on all major issues, national and international, and he strongly advocated cooperation among nations. His sane and progressive approach to economic and social problems placed him in ever-greater positions of responsibility in public service. His record of accomplishment was free from charges of political bias and colored every phase of American life. He firmly believed that military aggression was the greatest single danger in the world and was determined that America should at all times be so strong and so well prepared that no power would dare risk aggression. He deplored economic hardship in a land of plenty, and proposed to utilize the country's resources to thwart future depressions. Labor made important strides forward and production thrived under his leadership.

A champion of civil rights during his years on the Bench, Warren demanded a broad interpretation of constitutional protection of the individual. He frequently wrote the Court's majority decision, perhaps most notably in such cases as the historic *Brown v. Board of Education of Topeka* in 1952. Chief Justice Warren wrote the Court's unanimous opinion, outlawing racial segregation in the public schools. Reactions ranged from public hostility toward the Court on the part of some Americans to complete acceptance by others. Thus an established doctrine of many years was destroyed, paving the way for much of the civil rights legislation of the fifties and sixties.

Another of the many emotional questions that reached the Warren Court was whether children could or had to participate in daily prayer in the public schools. The Court ruled that no state or local authority could enforce daily Bible readings or the reciting of the Lord's Prayer. The outcome was based on earlier decisions requiring the separation of church and state. In effect, the Warren Court ruled against public prayer in any schools which children were compelled by law to attend. The fourteenth Chief Justice wrote another memorable opinion stating that a person taken into custody in a criminal case has the right to legal counsel and at all times must be advised of his constitutional rights to remain silent and that, after proper advice, the individual may waive these rights, although he may demand these rights to silence and counsel at any subsequent time. He also wrote the opinion that the states must apportion both houses of their legislatures on the basis of population. The "Warren Report" of the investigation into the assassination of John F. Kennedy was written under his supervision.

The only man to be elected to a third term as governor of California, Earl Warren resigned that office in order to head the Supreme Court in 1953. He was an influential leader of the Judiciary, a conservative who became a liberal. His decisions reflected a concern for fairness and justice more than absolute precision and brought him both praise and condemnation. Warren firmly believed that people should respect the decisions of the Court once they were handed down. Before he released an opinion, he checked every detail and made certain that no small yet vital point of law that might alter or destroy its purpose had been overlooked. To the Chief Justice, differences were something that could always be worked out, and troubles were only problems that had yet to be solved. His influence touched the life of the nation more than that of most Presidents. The controversies surrounding the civil rights and criminal law decisions, the voting rights and civil liberties cases, the prayer rulings—and the claim by some in the field of law that the Warren Court was motivated by politics in its legal philosophy—made Earl Warren an opponent of judicial and political conservatives and an enemy of the far right, especially the John Birch Society, which began the "Impeach Warren" crusade. It never got past the publicity stage.

The law was Warren's first and enduring interest, and as its guardian, he made secure his place in history. Along with Charles Evans Hughes and John Marshall, he has been ranked by some among the greatest Chief Justices. His critics disagree, as might the man himself, but, whether one agrees with his decisions or not, by any standard, Chief Justice Earl Warren made his mark on his time.

Warren Earl Burger was nominated by President Richard M. Nixon to succeed Earl Warren as Chief Justice of the Supreme Court in 1969. After his Senate confirmation, the judicial oath was administered to him on June 24. Although he was a first-rate legal craftsman, his nomination surprised many observers, since he was virtually an unknown to most Americans. Predictions about the new Chief Justice were reserved. Burger was looked upon as a conservative, and many people viewed his nomination as an attempt by President Nixon to reverse the pattern of liberalism which had been set by the Warren Court, especially in the area of criminal justice. The new head of the Supreme Court was known to be a defender of judicial control and deeply interested in Court and prison reform. Members of the Court, both conservatives and liberals, approved of the appointment of the man from Minnesota, anticipating the creation of a more moderate and less activist majority in the high Court for the first time in twenty years.

Before being appointed to the Supreme Court Bench, Warren Burger had served in the Justice Department as an Assistant Attorney General and had represented the United States government as a member of and legal consultant with the International Labor Organization at Geneva, during the Eisenhower administration. While he was a judge on the Court of Appeals for the District of Columbia, his ideas involving criminal justice often clashed with those of his more liberal colleagues. He challenged the decision handed down by the Supreme Court limiting the rights of the police to interrogate suspects. He said that many of the rules were unrealistic and almost impossible to administer. Nevertheless, he praised some opinions of the Judiciary as masterpieces of law based on fundamental American principles.

A strict constructionist, the fifteenth Chief Justice considers a fair balance between the rights of the individual and the needs of society to be the pinnacle of justice. He firmly believes that the rights of society take precedence over those of the individual. Although Burger is in agreement with most of the decisions of the Warren Court, he has frequently criticized his predecessor's rulings on the rights of defendants in criminal cases. From the beginning, it has been evident through his dissents from the majority that new attitudes on cases involving crime, the abortion laws, labor picketing, and obscenity would come from the Burger Court.

Off the Bench, the Chief Justice has been more outspoken in his disagreements with the opinions of the Court than Earl Warren ever was. In frequent speeches, he has used the prestige of his office to promote prison reform, and he has set up training programs for court administrators. In a few significant cases he has criticized Court rulings on free speech, dissent, and capital punishment.

Some of his colleagues were at first disappointed with his low-keyed persuasion and believed that the Burger Court would be slow in its development. However, within a few years, the decisions of Chief Justice Burger have had a definite impact upon our courts, especially in the field of criminal law.

The duties of his high office have sometimes been difficult, often rewarding. In October 1973, the Chief Justice administered the oath of office to the nation's first foreign-born Secretary of State, Henry A. Kissinger.

On December 6, 1973, two months after the resignation of Spiro T. Agnew, Burger swore into office the fortieth Vice-President of the United States, Gerald Rudolph Ford, the first man to have his appointment confirmed to that office by the Congress under the Twenty-fifth Amendment, Section 2, which states, "Whenever there is a vacancy in the office of the

Vice-President, the President shall nominate a Vice-President who shall take office upon confirmation by a majority vote of both Houses of Congress." Eight months later, on August 9, 1974, Chief Justice Burger administered the oath of office to the thirty-eighth President of the United States, Gerald R. Ford. And on January 20, 1977, he swore in the thirty-ninth President, James Earl Carter.

Warren Earl Burger may well be, if the need arises in the future, the Chief Justice who writes Supreme Court decisions of great national and international consequence. His judicial rulings could involve the energy crisis, food shortage, drug abuse, pollution, minority rights, civil liberties, criminal justice, capital punishment, and safeguards against misuse of public power. However, he always preferred that the Supreme Court take a lesser role than during the Warren years. In addition, he has questioned the readiness of the Court to intervene in problems that he feels are better left to the Legislative branch of government. It is too soon to determine what historic impact his judicial opinions will produce. A more precise profile of Warren Burger will ultimately be determined by the people, the times, and the issues resolved by his Court.

Each Chief Justice, in his dedicated career, prepares his own place in history. If there is one conclusion and truth to be reached about the prestigious Chief Justiceship, it is that the one at the top must project all the qualifications of the other Justices in character, knowledge of the law, intelligence, and above all else, leadership and readiness for increased responsibility on the most powerful Court in the world.

Part Two

Landmark Decisions

THE CONSTITUTION OF THE UNITED STATES was written nearly two hundred years ago. It spells out the rights of the Federal government, the rights of the states, and the rights of individuals. It tells us how our government is formed and outlines the specific powers of each section of that government. The Amendments to the Constitution further explain our rights and the limitations on those rights. But as you read the following cases, you will see that there are different ways of looking at the same principle and different ways of interpreting what at first glance seems perfectly clear.

To get an idea of how complex this becomes, let us imagine that we are justices of the Supreme Court and that we are making decisions stemming from an Amendment that says "the State shall not restrict the right of any man to drink milk." This sentence seems very simple, until we get our first case, *Johnson v. State X*.

Ms. Johnson argues that the State has passed a discriminatory law prohibiting women from drinking milk. The State argues that the law reads only that no "man" can be restricted from drinking milk. How would you rule? You could rule that the term "man" included women as well. You could also rule that it did not and leave it up to the Congress to pass an Amendment that would include women.

Our next case is *Jones v. State X*. Mr. Jones says that he doesn't have any milk to drink because State X allowed the Udderly Fantastic Milk Co. to raise its prices to a level that Jones cannot afford. The State argues that it's not responsible for the fact that Jones doesn't have the money to buy milk. How would you rule? Does Jones's right to drink milk also include a requirement that the State provide him with milk if he cannot afford it? Or does Jones's right to drink milk only mean that he has the right to drink milk if he can get it? You will see in some of the actual cases below that the Court has interpreted the right to counsel as meaning that the state has to provide counsel in criminal cases if the defendant cannot afford it.

Our next case will be the *State v. Board of Education*. The Board of Education argues that because the State provides money for a school lunch program in one district and because milk is included in the lunch program, therefore milk has to be provided for all children in all the school districts, for otherwise there is a restriction on those children not provided with milk. The State argues that providing milk for some children is not equivalent to restricting others. How would you rule? You could rule that there is no "right to milk" and that the State is acting within its rights. You could rule, however, that once milk is provided by a public institution, it can be considered a right according to State law or by tradition, and that the denial of milk to some children then violates the Milk Amendment.

You might later decide that you were wrong and reverse your decision. A later court might decide that you were wrong to change your decision and bring back your original decision.

If it were suddenly discovered that some milk contained harmful contaminants, you might have to consider limitations on the right to drink milk in order to protect public safety.

If one company controlled all the cows in the country and raised the price of milk, would that be a restriction of the right to drink milk? Since the Amendment states merely that "no State" has the right to restrict the drinking of milk, would you refuse to hear the case on the grounds that a State has not violated the conditions of the Amendment? These are only a sample of the type of difficulties you might face if you were a Supreme Court Justice. You will see in the cases that follow that the Court has tackled many problems whose principles are similar to those of our milk cases. The cases below were selected because the decisions handed down by the Court were particularly significant in some way or another either in interpreting the Constitution or in extending or limiting our rights as citizens of the United States.

Slaughterhouse Cases *1873*

The Supreme Court upheld a Louisiana law granting a monopoly on slaughterhouses. The decision further defined the rights of citizens under the Amendments, but left the bulk of civil rights law under state jurisdiction.

Civil Rights Cases *1883*

The Court held that the Fourteenth Amendment empowered Congress to protect national citizenship rights only in cases where *states* had denied such rights. The denial of rights by private citizens was not protected by Congress. This meant, in effect, that the state could not pass a law denying the rights of a citizen, but if the rights of the citizen were denied by individuals within a state, the Court had no jurisdiction.

Norfolk & Western R. Co. v. Pennsylvania *1890*

The Court held that a tax on interstate rail transportation was a burden on interstate commerce, and was therefore invalid.

United States v. E.C. Knight & Co. *1895*

The Court held that that combination, which had been formed to control the sugar supply of the nation, was not in restraint of interstate commerce. This interpretation of the Sherman Anti-Trust Act limited its application to the transportation aspects of the Act rather than the manufacturing aspects.

Gibson v. Mississippi   *1896*

The Court held that, although states could not exclude blacks
from juries simply because of their color, other grounds which
effectively removed blacks from juries were not a denial of
rights. It became illegal to exclude a black person from a jury
because he was black, but it was valid to exclude all people
whose grandfathers had not been eligible to vote. In 1896 the
grandfathers of most black people had been slaves and not
eligible to vote, so that black people were in effect excluded by
such a rule.

Plessy v. Ferguson   *1896*

The decision upheld a Louisiana law segregating facilities on
railroad passenger trains. This decision, that segregated
facilities did not violate constitutional rights as long as there
were "equal" facilities, established the "separate but equal" doctrine, which was to stand for many years. It led to dual facilities
in many places. Thus it was not unusual to see two water foun-
tains, one marked "white" and one marked "colored," or two
sets of restrooms similarly marked.

DeLima v. Bidwell   *1901*

The Court held that, with the end of the Spanish-American
War, Puerto Rico ceased to be a foreign country and that its
products were no longer subject to import duties without express Congressional authority.

Loewe v. Lawlor   *1908*

The Court held that when a labor union is engaged in a
secondary boycott, the union's activities fall within the Sherman
Anti-Trust Act. A union picketing a hat manufacturer with
whom it had a direct grievance would be engaged in a primary
boycott. If that same union picketed stores that sold the hats
and that were not directly connected with the manufacturer, it
would be engaged in a secondary boycott.

Berea College v. Kentucky *1908*

The state of Kentucky had granted an educational charter for the formation of a school that would educate both black and white students. A Kentucky state law specified that all education must be segregated. The Court upheld this law on the grounds that the rights of blacks were not being violated as long as they were being given equal education.

Bailey v. Alabama *1911*

The Court held invalid a state law requiring debtors to "work out" what they owed to creditors the law was found to be in conflict with the Thirteenth Amendment.

Weeks v. United States *1914*

The Court held for the first time that evidence secured through an illegal search was invalid in Federal courts under the provisions of the Fourth Amendment.

Caminetti v. United States *1917*

The Mann (White Slave) Act had specifically outlawed forcing any woman to commit an immoral act for commercial purposes. In *Caminetti v. United States* the Court broadened the ruling to mean that prosecutions needed only to prove that women were forced to commit an immoral act and not that there was a financial transaction involved as well.

Adams v. Tanner *1917*

The ruling invalidated a Washington state law forbidding employment agencies to collect fees from job seekers. The Court found that the state was depriving the agencies of a property right (in this case the right to conduct a business) without due process of law.

Goldman v. United States   *1918*

This ruling sustained the right of the United States to compel military service. The Court ruled that compulsory military service was not an unreasonable infringement upon individual liberty.

Abrams v. United States   *1919*

The Court held that the advocacy of strikes at plants engaged in manufacturing war materials amounted to a "clear and present danger." Under this concept, fundamental rights normally protected by the Constitution could be limited. Justice Holmes made a noteworthy objection to this ruling on the grounds that it constituted in effect a limitation of ideas.

Leser v. Garnett   *1922*

The Court rejected the state of Maryland's contention that the Nineteenth Amendment, which gave women the right to vote, should be struck down because it arbitrarily added to the state's electorate and thus destroyed its political balance.

United States v. Lanza   *1922*

The Fifth Amendment to the Constitution states that no person can be put in jeopardy more than once for the same crime. This means that if a person is tried and acquitted of a crime, and is therefore released from the danger of being punished for that crime, he cannot again be brought to trial for that same crime. The Court, in *United States v. Lanza,* held that this protection held only for a second prosecution in the Federal courts and did not cover a separate state trial.

Adkins v. Children's Hospital   *1923*

In this decision the court invalidated a District of Columbia minimum wage law for women as an infringement of freedom of contract under the Fifth Amendment.

Pierce v. Society of Sisters *1925*

The Court struck down a state law which would have prohibited private school education by compelling all children to attend public school.

Aldridge v. United States *1931*

Aldridge, a black man, was tried for the murder of a white man. Aldridge raised the issue of possible racial prejudice during the examination of jurors. The Court ruled that he had a right to do this, as it might have a bearing on the verdict issued. The Court thereby recognized the fact that racial prejudice existed and could affect the outcome of a trial involving people of different racial background.

Near v. Minnesota *1931*

The state of Minnesota had a law which authorized closing publications alleged to be guilty of false charges against public officials. The Minnesota law suggested that a public official could have a newspaper, magazine or other publication shut down unless it could prove that the charges made against the public official were true. The Court decided that this was a violation of the publication's freedom of speech. Although a public official can sue a publication and try to collect damages for false accusations, he cannot seek to have the publication closed down.

Nixon v. Condon *1932*

Political parties in Texas placed limitations on who could and could not vote in primaries in that state, with the result that only whites could vote. The Court ruled that this was a violation of the Fourteenth Amendment.

Powell v. Alabama *1932*

The Court ruled that any defendant had a right, under the Fourteenth Amendment, to legal counsel in felony cases.

Norris v. Alabama   *1935*

The conviction of a black defendant was set aside when it was demonstrated that blacks were consistently barred from both the grand jury and the trial jury. The barring of blacks from the grand jury and the trial jury was cited as a prejudicial procedure which created an atmosphere in which the rights of the accused could not be fully protected.

Grosjean v. American Press Co.   *1936*

An advertising tax was levied on newspapers in the state of Louisiana. The tax was construed by the Court to be a method of controlling or affecting the content of the papers and, therefore, to be an unconstitutional infringement on the freedom of the press.

Brown v. Mississippi   *1936*

The Court ruled that a conviction based on a coerced confession was invalid. This meant that if a suspect was beaten, threatened, bribed, or in any way forced or improperly persuaded to confess, then a conviction stemming from that confession would be illegal. The decision prevents the police in the United States from torturing suspects to make them confess to crimes that they did not commit.

Lovell v. Griffin   *1938*

A Georgia city ordinance, aimed primarily at Jehovah's Witnesses, stated that it was necessary to obtain a license before distributing literature in the streets. The Court held this ordinance invalid under the First Amendment.

Missouri ex rel. Gaines v. Canada   *1938*

The Court gave the opinion that a state offering higher education to white students had to offer similar educational opportunities to black students. This put a burden on the states that wished to maintain segregated facilities and was one of the Court's earliest steps toward abolishing the "separate but equal" doctrine.

Lane v. Wilson *1939*

In 1915 the Court had held invalid Oklahoma's so-called grandfather clause, which restricted voting rights to persons whose grandfathers had been eligible to vote, that is, blacks, whose grandfathers had of course been slaves, were not allowed to vote. The Court now ruled this and all other state laws which denied equal opportunity to voters of all races to be unconstitutional under the Fifteenth Amendment.

Nardone v. United States *1939*

The decision affirmed the Communications Act of 1934 making any evidence obtained by wiretapping illegal.

Minersville School District v. Gobitis *1940*

To most Americans, reciting the Pledge of Allegiance means that one vows to support the United States. To people of certain religious faiths, however, the swearing of allegiance to the United States is directly opposed to their belief that they can swear allegiance only to God. The Court ruled that the law did not attempt to promote or restrict religious beliefs and was therefore not violating the rights of the offended religious groups.

Georgia v. Taylor *1942*

The state of Georgia had a law whereby a person who owed money that he could not repay might be compelled to "work out" his debt by providing his services to the person to whom he owed the money. The Court declared this a violation of the Thirteenth Amendment.

Betts v. Brady 1942

The Court issued the opinion that the right to counsel for a defendant was not a constitutional right under the Sixth Amendment, but rather a policy supported only by specific laws. The Court therefore would not reverse the conviction of a man too poor to afford an attorney at his criminal trial.

McNabb v. United States 1943

The Court affirmed that an accused person must be taken before a judicial officer without delay following arrest. This prevents people from being held in jail for long periods of time without being formally charged with a crime.

West Virginia Board of Education v. Barnette 1943

This case overturned the *Gobitis* case and stated that the compulsory flag salute infringes upon the First Amendment guarantee of free exercise of religion.

Girouard v. United States 1946

The Court rejected the idea that foreign-born conscientious objectors, those who refused to fight in the army, were ineligible to become citizens of the United States. This meant that persons wishing to be naturalized could be even if they refused to participate in our wars.

Morgan v. Virginia 1946

This decision invalidated segregation laws which involved interstate travel. In other words, if a train traveled from one state to another, there could be no law which restricted the rights of any person on it because of race, creed, or color.

Everson v. Board of Education 1947

The Court upheld a New Jersey law permitting the state to reimburse the parents of school children for transportation to

John Jay, the first Chief Justice of the
United States Supreme Court (1789–1795)

Courtesy of the Library of Congress

The signing of the Constitution

Chief Justice John Marshall
(1801–1835)

Courtesy of the Library of Congress

Chief Justice Roger B. Taney
(1836–1864)

Courtesy of the Library of Congress

Chief Justice Charles E. Hughes
(1930–1941)
Courtesy of the Library of Congress

Chief Justice Earl Warren
(1953–1969)
Courtesy of the Library of Congress

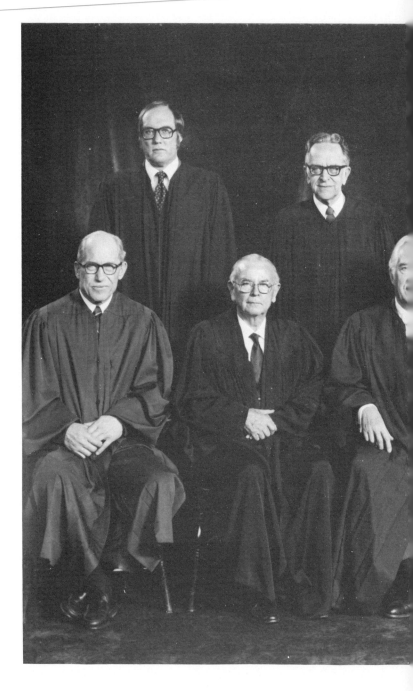

The current Court: *first row, from left,* Justice Byron R. White, Justice William J. Brennan, Jr., Chief Justice Warren E. Burger, Justice Potter Stewart, Justice

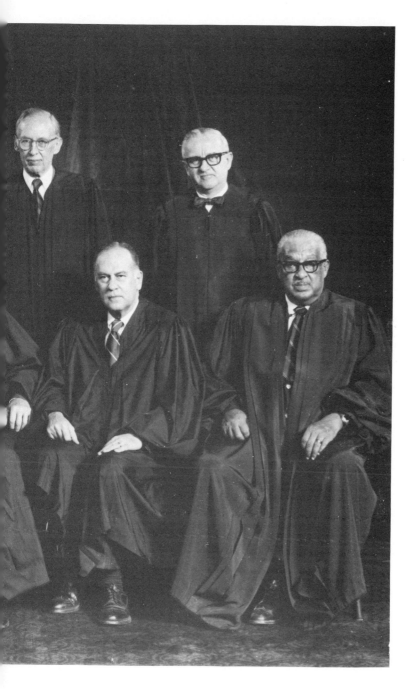

Thurgood Marshall; *second row, from left,* Justice
William H. Rehnquist, Justice Harry A. Blackmun, Justice Lewis F. Powell, Jr., Justice John P. Stevens

The Supreme Court Building

Courtesy of the Library of Congress

and from parochial school. The argument of the majority was supported by the First Amendment, which guarantees freedom of religion, and by the Fourteenth Amendment, which prohibits the passing of any state law which inhibits the rights of citizens under the Constitution. A law which forbad the reimbursement of transportation costs for children attending parochial schools while the state provided free transportation for those attending public schools would inhibit the rights of those going to parochial school.

Harris v. United States   *1947*

The Court said that the government had a right to seize illegal matter found during an authorized search of a suspect.

Illinois ex rel. McCollum v. Board of Education   *1948*

This decision invalidated state "released time" policy, under which public schools were being used to give religious instruction to those who chose it. The argument was that the use of public facilities for education which was essentially religious in nature and not purely educational was in violation of the First Amendment.

Shelley v. Kraemer   *1948*

The Court held that while racially restrictive rules might be valid between private parties to an agreement, they could not be enforced by state laws. It was all right, in other words, for people in a certain neighborhood to agree not to sell to members of a racial minority, but the state could not pass a law making it illegal to do so.

Terminiello v. Chicago   *1949*

The Court invalidated an ordinance which prohibited disturbances caused by provocative speech. The Court held that such an ordinance was a violation of the First Amendment.

American Communications Association v. Douds   *1950*

The Court upheld the provision in the Taft-Hartley Act which made all employees working under this act sign an affidavit stating that they were not Communists. The idea here was that the Congress has the power to protect the public interest from politically motivated strikes.

Sweatt v. Painter   *1950*

The Court ruled that a state university must admit qualified blacks when facilities in a segregated state university are not equal. This in effect forced states either to spend large amounts on their state educational budgets to upgrade segregated schools or to admit blacks to the "white" schools. Although the "separate but equal" doctrine had been affirmed previously by the Court, the actual "equality" was rarely examined. So long as a state had nominally equal facilities—if a restroom, for example, was provided for blacks but was not kept in good repair or was not as accessible as the restroom for whites—the law was satisfied. The ruling in *Sweatt v. Painter* interpreted the law as meaning equal to white facilities in substance.

Feiner v. New York   *1951*

Here the Court upheld the conviction of a person who refused to stop making provocative statements when authorities, reasonably believing that what he was saying would lead to violence, requested him to desist. The question here was whether we have unlimited rights of free speech under the First Amendment. The Court ruled that our right to freedom of speech is limited as it affects public safety. Thus the yelling of "Fire!" in a crowded theater when there is no fire is rightly punishable because the right of the public not to be endangered by what you say is greater than your right to say anything you wish. It must be shown, however, that there is a real and apparent danger in what you are saying before any limitations can be made on your freedom of speech.

Brown v. Board of Education   *1954*

The Court held that the "separate but equal" doctrine was unconstitutional. This meant that schools and other public
facilities which had segregated blacks and whites could no
longer do so. The ruling maintained that, although historically
the "separate but equal" doctrine might satisfy the rights
guaranteed by the Constitution, contemporary conditions
showed that the doctrine did not guarantee full rights for all
citizens. A later decision concerning the same case required the
states to proceed in the desegregation of schools with "all delib-
erate speed."

Yates v. United States   *1957*

The Smith Act had made it a crime to advocate the overthrow
of the government. The Court ruled that to come under the law
the advocacy must be overt action and not merely abstract argument. It would be a crime to advocate storming the White
House and Congress, and physically overthrowing the government, but it would not be a crime to try to convince people to
overthrow the government by peaceful means or simply to say
that the government should be overthrown without actually
suggesting overt action.

Roth v. United States   *1957*

The Court held that laws against obscenity do not infringe
upon the constitutional rights guaranteed by the First Amendment. The Court suggested that the test of whether or not
material was obscene was its appeal to "prurient interests."

Henry v. United States   *1959*

The Court set aside the conviction of a man for possession of
stolen goods. Federal agents had stopped the defendant's car to
search for illicit liquor and unexpectedly come upon the stolen
goods.

Burton v. Wilmington Pkg. Authority   *1961*

The Court ruled that a restaurant's policy of not serving blacks was invalid under the Fourteenth Amendment if the restaurant was licensed by a public agency.

Torcaso v. Watkins   *1961*

The decision overruled an old Maryland law requiring officeholders to swear that they believe in God. The law was deemed contrary to the freedom of religion clause in the First Amendment.

Chewning v. Cunningham   *1962*

The ruling invalidated a conviction based on a trial without counsel.

Engle v. Vitale   *1962*

The Court ruled that the anti-establishment clause of the First Amendment prohibits a state from composing any prayer or other expression of religious attitude for use in public schools. Such practices as "moments of silent prayer" therefore would be outlawed by this ruling.

Gideon v. Wainwright   *1963*

The Court ruled that under the equal protection clause of the Fourteenth Amendment, counsel had to be provided for indigent defendants in all criminal proceedings.

Wright v. Georgia   *1963*

The Court set aside a conviction of blacks ordered to leave a public park by a police officer. The park was normally used by whites only. The Court held that, in ordering the blacks to leave the park, the police officer was ordering them to give up part of their constitutional rights.

Jacobellis v. Ohio *1964*

The Court ruled that a work is not obscene unless it is "utterly devoid of redeeming social importance."

Escobedo v. Illinois *1964*

The Court ruled that the right to counsel begins to take effect when a police investigation focuses on a specific suspect. In other words, police may question people regarding the commission or circumstances of a crime, but when a person actually becomes a suspect, that person has the right to counsel, and the police must inform him of his rights before any questioning takes place.

Pointer v. Texas *1965*

The Court held that in criminal cases a defendant had the right not only to have counsel, but also to confront and cross-examine witnesses against him.

Griswold v. Connecticut *1965*

The Court struck down a Connecticut law prohibiting the use of contraceptives, holding that enforcement of the law against married couples infringed on the right of marital privacy, protected by the Bill of Rights.

Shepard v. Maxwell *1966*

The Court reversed the conviction in a sensational murder trial because the publicity at and attending the trial proceedings was such that it prejudiced the defendant's right to a fair and impartial trial.

Miranda v. Arizona *1966*

The Court held that a suspect had the right to counsel during interrogation and that the interrogators had to inform him of his rights prior to asking him any questions.

Katz v. United States 1967

The Court ruled that a recording obtained through an electronic eavesdropping device placed on top of public telephone booth by FBI agents, without a search warrant, was inadmissible as evidence. Prior to this decision, the Fourth Amendment had been considered to apply only to invasion of privacy through physical trespass. In this case the Court held that the Fourth Amendment also protects reasonable expectations of privacy.

In re Gault 1967

The Court extended the right to counsel and the privilege against self-incrimination to juvenile courts.

Board of Education v. Allen 1968

The Court upheld a New York State program providing free textbook loans to private as well as public school students. This decision broadened the area of permissible state aid to parochial school students.

Terry v. Ohio 1968

The Court held, with some limitations, that a "stop and frisk" law was constitutionally permissible.

Tinker v. Des Moines Independent Community School District 1969

In this case the Court held for the first time that the right of free speech guaranteed by the Constitution limits state power to prohibit political protest by students in secondary schools. The Court ruled that a public secondary school's ban on the wearing of black arm bands as a protest against the Vietnam war was in violation of the First and Fourteenth Amendments.

Shapiro v. Thompson 1969

The Court declared unconstitutional state laws making welfare assistance conditional on one-year state residence. The Court held that these laws violated the Fourteenth Amendment by infringing upon the welfare recipient's constitutional right to travel.

Chimel v. California   *1969*

The Court held that, under the Fourteenth Amendment, a warrantless search accompanying a defendant's arrest in his home may not extend beyond the area where he might reach to obtain a weapon or destroy evidence.

Benton v. Maryland   *1969*

The Court ruled that the double jeopardy clause of the Fifth Amendment also applies to states, through the Fourteenth Amendment. This ruling overturned *United States v. Lanza* (1922).

In re Winship   *1970*

This decision requires that conviction of a criminal defendant be based on proof of guilt "beyond a reasonable doubt." The Court also ruled that the same standard must apply to juvenile-court delinquency proceedings.

Wyman v. James   *1971*

In this case the Court held that an AFDC (Aid to Families with Dependent Children) recipient may not refuse a warrantless home visit without risking termination of benefits, since the visit cannot be considered a search because its purpose is not to investigate criminal law violations.

Harris v. New York   *1971*

The Court held that a defendant's statement obtained without the necessary *Miranda* warnings is admissible for the purpose of impeaching his testimony at his trial, even though it is inadmissible as part of the prosecution's case.

Swann v. Charlotte-Mecklenburg Board of Education   *1971*

In this case the Supreme Court defined the powers of Federal district courts in the struggle to eliminate all traces of state-imposed school segregation. The Court ruled that district courts may use racial quotas as guidelines, rezone school attendance districts, and order bus transportation of students.

New York Times Co. v. United States   *1971*

In this case the Court refused the Nixon administration's demand that it prohibit publication of the "Pentagon Papers" by the *New York Times* and the *Washington Post.* The Court held that the government had failed to meet the heavy burden of justification prescribed by *Near v. Minnesota* (1931) in order to sustain a prior restraint upon publication.

Eisenstadt v. Baird   *1972*

The Court declared unconstitutional a Massachusetts law which prohibited all distribution of contraceptives except when made by registered physicians and pharmacists to married persons. The Court held that in allowing the distribution of contraceptives to married persons but not to unmarried persons, the law violated the equal-protection clause of the Fourteenth Amendment. This decision extended *Griswold v. Connecticut's* protection of married persons to unmarried persons as well.

Furman v. Georgia   *1972*

The Court ruled that imposing the death penalty in crimes for which it is not mandatory constitutes cruel and unusual punishment, which violates the Eighth and Fourteenth Amendments.

Roe v. Wade and *Doe v. Bolton*   *1973*

In these cases the Court ruled that the Texas and Georgia laws regulating abortion violated the due process clause of the Fourteenth Amendment. The Court held that women's interest falls within the zone of privacy protected by the Constitution, and that state interests justify only limited interference by the government.

Frontiero v. Richardson *1973*

The Court overturned Federal statutes permitting servicemen to claim their wives as dependents without showing actual dependency but requiring servicewomen to prove the dependency of their husbands. The Court held that these statutes violated the due process clause of the Fifth Amendment.

Gertz v. Robert Welch, Inc. *1974*

In this case the Court held that although public figures and public officials must prove recklessness in order to recover damages in defamation suits against the news media, private individuals only need to prove negligence.

United States v. Nixon *1974*

The Supreme Court ruled that the Presidential privilege of Executive confidentiality must give way to the need for evidence in a criminal trial.

Milliken v. Bradley *1974*

The Court ruled that Federal courts cannot order multidistrict remedies for school segregation without proof that school-district lines have been drawn in a discriminatory manner or that discriminatory acts of one or more school districts or state officials have caused interdistrict segregation. This decision limits the power of Federal courts to treat largely black urban school districts and largely white suburban districts as a single unit in ordering desegregation plans.

Taylor v. Louisiana *1975*

The Court declared unconstitutional a Louisiana law that excluded all women from jury duty unless they filed written declarations of their desire to be eligible. The Court held that this law deprived criminal defendants of their right to a trial by an impartial jury drawn from a fair cross section of the community.

Goss v. Lopez   *1975*

The Court struck down an Ohio statue giving public school principals authority to suspend students for up to ten days without a hearing. The Court held that State-guaranteed public education is a constitutionally protected property interest of which students cannot be deprived without notice and a hearing.

Weinberger v. Wiesenfeld   *1975*

The Court declared unconstitutional the Social Security Act provision that provides widows but not widowers with survivors' benefits while caring for minor children.

City of Richmond v. United States   *1975*

In this case the Court considered for the first time whether an annexation which changed a city's racial composition violated the Voting Rights Act of 1965. The Court ruled that a city of mixed racial composition can annex a white suburb if there are legitimate reasons for the annexation and if the city employs a ward election system reflecting the voting strength of the black community.

Nebraska Press Association v. Stuart   *1976*

The Supreme Court unanimously struck down a court order prohibiting press coverage of confessions and other information about the defendant in a sensational murder case. This was the first time the Court considered the constitutionality of prior restraint upon publication in such cases. The majority opinion indicated that such orders would be upheld only under the most extraordinary circumstances.

Afterword

Today and Tomorrow

EARLY IN OUR HISTORY, the Supreme Court of the United States was entrusted with the authority to make certain that men endowed with great power obeyed the laws, and the Court accepted the responsibility of changing established rules when the need was great. Wisdom is the keystone of any system of government which guarantees life and justice for its people. Therefore the men of the Judiciary branch of the government must possess extraordinary integrity, intelligence, and undaunted courage to seek out the truth.

The power of the Court must also be watched and controlled, and this is accomplished through new appointments to the Bench and through impeachment, if necessary, of members. Although the high Court does not directly change confirmed policy or write laws or exert Executive privileges, its great power is supported by the Constitution and by "the consent of the governed"; that is, the authority of the Court depends upon public acceptance of and respect for its judicial decisions. Unless the Court bases its decisions on sound reasons, its authority is in jeopardy. In the end, the power and authority of the Supreme Court depend upon the logic of its opinions.

All kinds of petitions come before the Supreme Court. Once the Bench has delivered its verdict, there can be no more appeals on a petition, for the Court's decisions are final. The Court may rule on any case that involves a constitutional dispute, such as school integration or the right to vote. This permits the Court to keep the Constitution and the nation abreast of new ideas and social reforms. Sometimes, however, the Court has delayed progress by clinging to outdated traditions.

The Constitution never changes, but the Justices who interpret it do. The historic document would become obsolete if from time to time the Court did not alter its interpretations and overturn some of its own decisions. Flexible interpretation by the Supreme Court has allowed the Constitution to grow with the country and with the times.

Despite the continuity of the Supreme Court, there have been occasional collisions of new and old Justices and new and old ideas throughout its history. This kind of diversity has made the future course of the Judiciary always extremely difficult to predict. All that is certain is that the Supreme Court of today is confronted with constitutional challenges as basic to our way of life as those faced in any Court session of the past. By the way these vital issues are decided, the true character of each Justice and of each Court will eventually be revealed.

The Supreme Court frequently has produced great drama and intense emotion in its process of defining the supreme law of the land. In dealing with constitutional questions, the Court is always free to change its mind and overrule past judgments when they fail to achieve their basic purpose. Although confusion, anger, and dispute are often the result of such Court procedures, this revision of ideas and principles has allowed the Constitution to grow and provide for each successive generation's needs.

The Supreme Court of the United States is one of the most powerful branches of governmental authority in the world. The provisions in the Constitution which invest the judicial power of the United States in one Supreme Court and such lower courts as the Congress might deem essential, and which specify the areas of jurisdiction for each, are defined very briefly in Article III. The only checks upon the Court specified by the Constitution are that the President nominates the Justices, that confirmation by the Senate is required, and that life-appointed Justices can be removed from the Bench only by impeachment for adequate cause or reason. An unofficial but sometimes very effective check lies also in public criticism and comment.

The high Court has long been a vital and effective arm of government in America. Its conduct and thinking have been shaped and tempered by constant pressures from numerous forces. From its very beginning, the Court has been dependent upon the Congress for legislation that will contribute form and essence to it. Much of this policy was established in the Judiciary Act of 1789. In order to work properly, the Court must also rely upon the Congress for its monetary compensation and proper assembly space. Although the present far-reaching powers of the Supreme Court are a direct result of its own conduct, its birth and continued life are rooted partly in political soil. The right of the Court to say what law is a just law by means of judicial review has established a distinct new body of laws which the country must obey. This judicial power is extraordinary, since it is not spelled out in the Constitution, and yet it has remained in effect throughout the years. At the same time, it has also been the basis of most judicial conflict with the Executive and Legislative branches of government and with state powers.

Although by its actions the Supreme Court represents the judicial authority of the nation, the Court alone cannot maintain the tradition of equal justice under the law. The American citizen who appreciates and demands freedom must keep informed about the actions and decisions of the highest Court in the land. In this way, we can all help to safeguard our birthright of liberty. The freedom, the diversity, and the greatness of our country are thus assured.

As long as the Supreme Court remains the living voice of the Constitution, our precious liberties cannot be lost by any American citizen, nor can the Court itself avoid clarification of what constitutes the law. Discussion of Court opinions by the people leads to public criticism, good and bad, and generally obliges the Justices to provide clear reasons for their decisions, in order to perpetuate our acceptance of just law. In the aftermath of many controversial opinions, however, the Supreme Court is often seen as a center of national dispute.

A few times in its history, the Judiciary branch of government has forced the Executive branch, that is, the President of the United States, to conform to its interpretation of the law. Long before its 1974 order that Richard Nixon surrender some sixty-four Watergate tapes and other data, the Court issued a subpoena ordering President Thomas Jefferson to appear before the Bench with certain documents needed in the treason trial of Aaron Burr in 1802. Jefferson denied that the Court held power over him and his actions as President, but he eventually submitted to the Court's demand.

By far the most outstanding test of endurance between a President and the Supreme Court occurred in the 1930s, when many of the New Deal programs of Franklin D. Roosevelt's administration were declared unconstitutional in majority rulings by the Court. Roosevelt responded by denouncing the Justices as "nine old men" and by introducing his "court-packing" plan to increase their number in order to gain a majority. His plan to enlarge the Court failed, but before the 1930s ended, the high Court had begun to adopt a stand more favorable to Roosevelt, and it upheld the Social Security Act and other legislation advocated by the President. Thirty years later, the Court forced the Congress to seat Adam Clayton Powell, ruling that the refusal to do so in 1967 by the House of Representatives was unconstitutional. Crisis in the Court has always passed.

The times, the people, new Justices, Court decisions, and public criticism combine to create a continuous check on the powers of the Supreme Court. Many believe that the members of the Court can be persuaded to change their ideas once they are subjected to widespread criticism. The Court is in no way exempt from social evolution, and it does remain part of a powerful and ever-changing democratic society. During the turbulent years of its existence, nations and empires have crumbled, but the United States, its faith, and its tribunal of justice have survived.

We can say that the Supreme Court has always in the past endured and survived the problems it had to meet and the hostile encounters it was subjected to, thereby making it the most self-reliant and one of the most dramatic segments of American government. In the increasing urgency of American life, what is more important is the future, not the history, of law and justice. Throughout its existence no other Court has struggled more than or risked so much as the Supreme Court of the United States in order to stay within its decreed limitations of power and still help transform law into justice.

The Supreme Court's workings cannot be left to the mercy of those over whom it has no control. The Court's role in government sometimes depends on public criticism and public acceptance. In order to safeguard justice for all, all of America should express the concern and interest that help an independent country to preserve and protect a national institution. A constant, careful scrutiny of each Justice and of the Court is demanded, and free criticism of all decisions is essential.

Every American must have the will to dedicate himself to the promotion and improvement of the administration of equal justice under law by the highest Court in the nation. With tolerance and patience and hope, the Supreme Court of today and tomorrow can turn the kindled spark of freedom into an eternal flame.

As all Americans must forever be alert to the exercise of power, they must also realize that justice depends upon the understanding and respect of the rights and the needs of others which are guaranteed by the Constitution and upheld by the Supreme Court.

Appendix A

The Constitution of the United States

PREAMBLE

We, the People of the United States, in Order to form a more perfect Union, establish Justice, insure domestic Tranquillity, provide for the common defence, promote the general Welfare, and secure the Blessings of Liberty to ourselves and our Posterity, do ordain and establish this Constitution for the United States of America.

ARTICLE I

Section 1. All legislative Powers herein granted shall be vested in a Congress of the United States, which shall consist of a Senate and House of Representatives.

Section 2. The House of Representatives shall be composed of Members chosen every second Year by the People of the several States, and the Electors in each State shall have the Qualifications requisite for Electors of the most numerous Branch of the State Legislature.

No Person shall be a Representative who shall not have attained to the age of twenty five Years, and been seven Years a

Citizen of the United States, and who shall not, when elected, be an Inhabitant of that State in which he shall be chosen.

Representatives and direct Taxes shall be apportioned among the several States which may be included within this Union, according to their respective Numbers, which shall be determined by adding to the whole Number of free Persons, including those bound to Service for a Term of Years, and excluding Indians not taxed, three fifths of all other Persons. The actual Enumeration shall be made within three Years after the first Meeting of the Congress of the United States, and within every subsequent Term of ten Years, in such Manner as they shall by Law direct. The Number of Representatives shall not exceed one for every thirty Thousand, but each State shall have at Least one Representative; and until such enumeration shall be made, the State of New Hampshire shall be entitled to chuse three, Massachusetts eight, Rhode-Island and Providence Plantations one, Connecticut five, New-York six, New Jersey four, Pennsylvania eight, Delaware one, Maryland six, Virginia ten, North Carolina five, South Carolina five, and Georgia three.

When vacancies happen in the Representation from any State, the Executive Authority thereof shall issue Writs of Election to fill such Vacancies.

The House of Representatives shall chuse their Speaker and other Officers; and shall have the sole Power of Impeachment.

Section 3. The Senate of the United States shall be composed of two Senators from each State, chosen by the Legislature thereof, for six Years; and each Senator shall have one Vote.

Immediately after they shall be assembled in Consequence of the first Election, they shall be divided as equally as may be into three Classes. The Seats of the Senators of the first Class shall be vacated at the Expiration of the second Year, of the second Class at the Expiration of the fourth Year, and of the third Class at the Expiration of the sixth Year, so that one third may be chosen every second Year; and if Vacancies happen by Resignation, or otherwise, during the Recess of the Legislature of any State, the Executive thereof may make temporary Appointments until the next Meeting of the Legislature, which shall then fill such Vacancies.

No Person shall be a Senator who shall not have attained to the Age of thirty Years, and been nine Years a Citizen of the United States, and who shall not, when elected, be an Inhabitant of that State for which he shall be chosen.

The Vice President of the United States shall be President of the Senate, but shall have no Vote, unless they be equally divided.

The Senate shall chuse their other Officers, and also a President pro tempore, in the Absence of the Vice President, or when he shall exercise the Office of President of the United States.

The Senate shall have the sole Power to try all Impeachments. When sitting for that Purpose, they shall be on Oath or Affirmation. When the President of the United States is tried the Chief Justice shall preside: And no Person shall be convicted without the Concurrence of two thirds of the Members present.

Judgment in Cases of Impeachment shall not extend further than to removal from Office, and disqualification to hold and enjoy any Office of honor, Trust or Profit under the United States: but the Party convicted shall nevertheless be liable and subject to Indictment, Trial, Judgment and Punishment, according to Law.

Section 4. The Times, Places and Manner of holding Elections for Senators and Representatives, shall be prescribed in each State by the Legislature thereof; but the Congress may at any time by Law make or alter such Regulations, except as to the Places of chusing Senators.

The Congress shall assemble at least once in every Year, and such Meeting shall be on the first Monday in December, unless they shall by Law appoint a different Day.

Section 5. Each House shall be the Judge of the Elections, Returns and Qualifications of its own Members, and a Majority of each shall constitute a Quorum to do Business; but a smaller Number may adjourn from day to day, and may be authorized to compel the Attendance of absent Members, in such Manner, and under such Penalties as each House may provide.

Each House may determine the Rules of its Proceedings, punish its Members for disorderly Behaviour, and, with the Concurrence of two thirds, expel a Member.

Each House shall keep a Journal of its Proceedings, and from time to time publish the same, excepting such Parts as may in their Judgment require Secrecy; and the Yeas and Nays of the Members of either House on any question shall, at the Desire of one fifth of those Present, be entered on the Journal.

Neither House, during the Session of Congress, shall, without the Consent of the other, adjourn for more than three days, nor to any other Place than that in which the two Houses shall be sitting.

Section 6. The Senators and Representatives shall receive a Compensation for their Services, to be ascertained by Law, and paid out of the Treasury of the United States. They shall in all Cases, except Treason, Felony and Breach of the Peace, be privileged from Arrest during their Attendance at the Session of their respective Houses, and in going to and returning from the same; and for any Speech or Debate in either House, they shall not be questioned in any other Place.

No Senator or Representative shall, during the Time for which he was elected, be appointed to any civil Office under the Authority of the United States, which shall have been created, or the Emoluments whereof shall have been encreased during such time; and no Person holding any Office under the United States, shall be a Member of either House during his Continuance in Office.

Section 7. All Bills for raising Revenue shall originate in the House of Representatives; but the Senate may propose or concur with amendments as on other Bills.

Every Bill which shall have passed the House of Representatives and the Senate, shall, before it become a Law, be presented to the President of the United States; If he approve he shall sign it, but if not he shall return it, with his Objections to that House in which it shall have originated, who shall enter the Objections at large on their Journal, and proceed to reconsider it. If after such Reconsideration two thirds of that House shall agree to pass the Bill, it shall be sent, together with the Objections, to the other House, by which it shall likewise be reconsidered, and if approved by two thirds of that House, it shall become a Law. But in all such Cases the Votes of both Houses shall be determined by Yeas and Nays, and the Names of the Persons voting for and against the Bill shall be entered on the Journal of each House respectively. If any Bill shall not be returned by the President within ten Days (Sunday excepted) after it shall have been presented to him, the Same shall be a Law, in like Manner as if he had signed it, unless the Congress by their Adjournment prevent its Return, in which Case it shall not be a Law.

Every Order, Resolution, or Vote to which the Concurrence of the Senate and House of Representatives may be necessary (except on a question of Adjournment) shall be presented to the President of the United States; and before the Same shall take Effect, shall be approved by him, or being disapproved by him, shall be repassed by two thirds of the Senate and House of Representatives, according to the Rules and Limitations prescribed in the Case of a Bill.

Section 8. The Congress shall have Power To lay and collect Taxes, Duties, Imposts and Excises, to pay the Debts and provide for the common Defence and the general Welfare of the United States; but all Duties, Imposts and Excises shall be uniform throughout the United States;

To borrow Money on the credit of the United States;

To regulate Commerce with foreign Nations, and among the several States, and with the Indian Tribes;

To establish an uniform Rule of Naturalization, and uniform laws on the subject of Bankruptcies throughout the United States;

To coin Money, regulate the Value thereof, and of foreign Coin, and fix the Standard of Weights and Measures;

To provide for the Punishment of counterfeiting the Securities and current Coin of the United States;

To establish Post Offices and post Roads;

To promote the Progress of Science and useful Arts, by securing for limited Times to Authors and Inventors the exclusive Right to their respective Writings and Discoveries;

To constitute Tribunals inferior to the supreme Court;

To define and punish Piracies and Felonies committed on the high Seas, and Offences against the Law of Nations;

To declare War, grant Letters of Marque and Reprisal, and make Rules concerning Captures on Land and Water;

To raise and support Armies, but no Appropriation of Money to that Use shall be for a longer Term than two Years;

To provide and maintain a Navy;

To make Rules for the Government and Regulation of the land and naval Forces;

To provide for calling forth the Militia to execute the Laws of the Union, suppress Insurrections and repel Invasions;

To provide for organizing, arming, and disciplining, the Militia, and for governing such Part of them as may be employed in the Service of the United States, reserving to the States respectively, the Appointment of the Officers, and the Authority of training the Militia according to the discipline pre-scribed by Congress;

To exercise exclusive Legislation in all Cases whatsoever, over such District (not exceeding ten Miles square) as may, by Cession of Particular States, and the Acceptance of Congress, become the Seat of the Government of the United States, and to exercise like Authority over all Places purchased by the Consent of the Legislature of the State in which the Same shall be, for the Erection of Forts, Magazines, Arsenals, dock-Yards, and other needful Buildings;—And

To make all Laws which shall be necessary and proper for carrying into Execution the foregoing Powers, and all other Powers vested by this Constitution in the Government of the United States, or in any Department or Officer thereof.

Section 9. The Migration or Importation of such Persons as any of the States now existing shall think proper to admit, shall not be prohibited by the Congress prior to the Year one thousand eight hundred and eight, but a Tax or duty may be imposed on such Importation, not exceeding ten dollars for each Person.

The Privilege of the Writ of Habeas Corpus shall not be suspended, unless when in Cases of Rebellion or Invasion the public Safety may require it.

No Bill of Attainder or ex post facto Law shall be passed.

No Capitation, or other direct, Tax shall be laid, unless in

Proportion to the Census of Enumeration herein before directed to be taken.

No Tax or Duty shall be laid on Articles exported from any State.

No Preference shall be given by any Regulation of Commerce or Revenue to the Ports of one State over those of another; nor shall Vessels bound to, or from, one State, be obliged to enter, clear or pay Duties in another.

No Money shall be drawn from the Treasury, but in Consequence of Appropriations made by Law; and a regular Statement and Account of the Receipts and Expenditures of all public Money shall be published from time to time.

No Title of Nobility shall be granted by the United States: And no Person holding any Office of Profit or Trust under them, shall, without the Consent of the Congress, accept of any present, Emolument, Office, or Title, of any kind whatever, from any King, Prince or foreign State.

Section 10. No State shall enter into any Treaty, Alliance, or Confederation; grant Letters of Marque and Reprisal; coin Money; emit Bills of Credit; make any Thing but gold and silver Coin a Tender in Payment of Debts; pass any Bill of Attainder, ex post facto Law, or Law impairing the Obligation of Contracts, or grant any Title of Nobility.

No State shall, without the Consent of the Congress, lay any Imposts or Duties on Imports or Exports, except what may be absolutely necessary for executing its inspection Laws: and the net Produce of all Duties and Imposts, laid by any State on Imports or Exports, shall be for the Use of the Treasury of the United States; and all such Laws shall be subject to the Revision and Controul of the Congress.

No State shall, without the Consent of Congress, lay any Duty of Tonnage, keep Troops, or Ships of War in time of Peace, enter into any Agreement or Compact with another State, or with a foreign Power, or engage in War, unless actually invaded, or in such imminent Danger as will not admit of delay.

ARTICLE II

Section 1. The executive Power shall be vested in a President of the United States of America. He shall hold his Office during the Term of four Years, and, together with the Vice President, chosen for the same Term, be elected, as follows:

Each State shall appoint, in such Manner as the Legislature thereof may direct, a Number of Electors, equal to the whole Number of Senators and Representatives to which the State may be entitled in the Congress: but no Senator or Representative, or Person holding an Office of Trust or Profit under the United States, shall be appointed an Elector.

The Electors shall meet in their respective States, and vote by Ballot for two Persons, of whom one at least shall not be an Inhabitant of the same State with themselves. And they shall make a List of all the Persons voted for, and of the Number of Votes for each; which List they shall sign and certify, and transmit sealed to the Seat of the Government of the United States, directed to the President of the Senate. The President of the Senate shall, in the Presence of the Senate and House of Representatives, open all the Certificates, and the Votes shall then be counted. The Person having the greatest Number of Votes shall be the President, if such Number be a Majority of the whole Number of Electors appointed; and if there be more than one who have such Majority, and have an equal Number of Votes, then the House of Representatives shall immediately chuse by Ballot one of them for President; and if no Person have a Majority, then from the five highest on the List the said House shall in like Manner chuse the President. But in chusing the President, the Votes shall be taken by States, the Representation from each State having one Vote; a quorum for this Purpose shall consist of a Member or Members from two thirds of the States, and a Majority of all the States shall be necessary to a Choice. In every Case, after the Choice of the President, the Person having the greatest Number of Votes of the Electors shall be the Vice President. But if there should remain two or more who have equal Votes, the Senate shall chuse from them by Ballot the Vice President.

The Congress may determine the Time of chusing the Electors, and the Day on which they shall give their Votes; which Day shall be the same throughout the United States.

No Person except a natural born Citizen, or a Citizen of the United States, at the time of the Adoption of this Constitution, shall be eligible to the Office of President; neither shall any person be eligible to that Office who shall not have attained to the Age of thirty five Years, and been fourteen Years a Resident within the United States.

In Case of the Removal of the President from Office, or of his Death, Resignation, or Inability to discharge the Powers and Duties of the said Office, the Same shall devolve on the Vice President, and the Congress may by Law provide for the Case of Removal, Death, Resignation or Inability, both of the President and Vice President, declaring what Officer shall then act as President, and such Officer shall act accordingly, until the Disability be removed, or a President shall be elected.

The President shall, at stated Times, receive for his Services, a Compensation, which shall neither be encreased nor diminished during the Period for which he shall have been elected, and he shall not receive within that Period any other Emolument from the United States, or any of them.

Before he enter on the Execution of his Office, he shall take the following Oath or Affirmation:—"I do solemnly swear (or affirm) that I will faithfully execute the Office of President of the United States, and will to the best of my Ability, preserve, protect and defend the Constitution of the United States."

Section 2. The President shall be Commander in Chief of the Army and Navy of the United States, and of the Militia of the several States, when called into the actual Service of the United States; he may require the Opinion, in writing, of the principal Officer in each of the executive Departments, upon any Subject relating to the Duties of their respective Offices, and he shall have Power to grant Reprieves and Pardons for Offenses against the United States, except in Cases of Impeachment.

He shall have Power, by and with the Advice and Consent of the Senate, to make Treaties, provided two thirds of the Senators present concur; and he shall nominate, and by and with the Advice and Consent of the Senate, shall appoint Ambassadors, other public Ministers and Consuls, Judges of the supreme Court, and all other Officers of the United States, whose Appointments are not herein otherwise provided for, and which shall be established by Law: but the Congress may by

Law vest the Appointment of such inferior Officers, as they think proper, in the President alone, in the Courts of Law, or in the Heads of Departments.

The President shall have Power to fill up all Vacancies that may happen during the Recess of the Senate, by granting Commissions which shall expire at the End of their next Session.

Section 3. He shall from time to time give to the Congress Information of the State of the Union, and recommend to their Consideration such Measures as he shall judge necessary and expedient; he may, on extraordinary Occasions, convene both Houses, or either of them, and in Case of Disagreement between them, with Respect to the Time of Adjournment, he may adjourn them to such Time as he shall think proper; he shall receive Ambassadors and other public Ministers; he shall take Care that the Laws be faithfully executed, and shall Commission all the Officers of the United States.

Section 4. The President, Vice President and all Civil Officers of the United States, shall be removed from Office on Impeachment for, and Conviction of, Treason, Bribery, or other high Crimes and Misdemeanors.

ARTICLE III

Section 1. The judicial Power of the United States, shall be vested in one supreme Court, and in such inferior Courts as the Congress may from time to time ordain and establish. The Judges, both of the supreme and inferior Courts, shall hold their Offices during good Behaviour, and shall, at stated Times, receive for their Services, a Compensation, which shall not be diminished during their Continuance in Office.

Section 2. The judicial Power shall extend to all Cases, in Law and Equity, arising under this Constitution, the Laws of the United States, and Treaties made, or which shall be made, under their Authority;—to all Cases affecting Ambassadors, other public Ministers and Consuls;—to all Cases of admiralty and maritime Jurisdiction;—to Controversies to which the United States shall be a Party;—to Controversies between two or more States;—between a State and Citizens of another

State;—between Citizens of different States;—between Citizens of the same State claiming Lands under Grants of different States, and between a State, or the Citizens thereof, and foreign States, Citizens or Subjects.

In all Cases affecting Ambassadors, other public Ministers and Consuls, and those in which a State shall be Party, the supreme Court shall have original Jurisdiction. In all the other Cases before mentioned, the supreme Court shall have appellate Jurisdiction, both as to Law and Fact, with such Exceptions, and under such Regulations as the Congress shall make.

The Trial of all Crimes, except in Cases of Impeachment, shall be by Jury; and such Trial shall be held in the State where the said Crimes shall have been committed; but when not committed within any State, the Trial shall be at such Place or Places as the Congress may by Law have directed.

Section 3. Treason against the United States, shall consist only in levying War against them, or in adhering to their Enemies, giving them Aid and Comfort. No Person shall be convicted of Treason unless on the Testimony of two Witnesses to the same overt Act, or on Confession in open Court.

The Congress shall have Power to declare the Punishment of Treason, but no Attainder of Treason shall work Corruption of Blood, or Forfeiture except during the Life of the Person attainted.

ARTICLE IV

Section 1. Full Faith and Credit shall be given in each State to the public Acts, Records, and judicial Proceedings of every other State. And the Congress may by general Laws prescribe the Manner in which such Acts, Records and Proceedings shall be proved, and the Effect thereof.

Section 2. The Citizens of each State shall be entitled to all Privileges and Immunities of Citizens in the several States.

A Person charged in any State with Treason, Felony, or other Crime, who shall flee from Justice, and be found in another State, shall on Demand of the executive Authority of the State from which he fled, be delivered up, to be removed to the State having Jurisdiction of the Crime.

No Person held to Service or Labour in one State, under the Laws thereof, escaping into another, shall, in Consequence of any Law or Regulation therein, be discharged from such Service or Labour, but shall be delivered up on Claim of the Party to whom such Service or Labour may be due.

Section 3. New States may be admitted by the Congress into this Union; but no new State shall be formed or erected within the Jurisdiction of any other State; nor any State be formed by the Junction of two or more States, or Parts of States, without the Consent of the Legislatures of the States concerned as well as of the Congress.

The Congress shall have Power to dispose of and make all needful Rules and Regulations respecting the Territory or other Property belonging to the United States; and nothing in this Constitution shall be so construed as to Prejudice any Claims of the United States, or of any particular State.

Section 4. The United States shall guarantee to every State in this Union a Republican Form of Government, and shall protect each of them against Invasion; and on Application of the Legislature, or of the Executive (when the Legislature cannot be convened) against domestic Violence.

ARTICLE V

The Congress, whenever two thirds of both Houses shall deem it necessary, shall propose Amendments to this Constitution, or, on the Application of the Legislatures of two thirds of the several States, shall call a Convention for proposing Amendments, which, in either Case, shall be valid to all Intents and Purposes, as Part of this Constitution, when ratified by the Legislatures of three fourths of the several States, or by Conventions in three fourths thereof, as the one or the other Mode of Ratification may be proposed by the Congress; Provided that no Amendment which may be made prior to the Year One thousand eight hundred and eight shall in any Manner affect the first and fourth Clauses in the Ninth Section of the first Article; and that no State, without its Consent, shall be deprived of its equal Suffrage in the Senate.

ARTICLE VI

All Debts contracted and Engagements entered into, before the Adoption of this Constitution, shall be as valid against the United States under this Constitution, as under the Confederation.

This Constitution, and the Laws of the United States which shall be made in Pursuance thereof; and all Treaties made, or which shall be made, under the Authority of the United States, shall be the supreme Law of the Land; and the Judges in every State shall be bound thereby, any Thing in the Constitution or Laws of any State to the Contrary notwithstanding.

The Senators and Representatives before mentioned, and the Members of the several State Legislatures, and all executive and judicial Officers, both of the United States and of the several States, shall be bound by Oath or Affirmation, to support this Constitution; but no religious Test shall ever be required as a Qualification to any Office or public Trust under the United States.

ARTICLE VII

The Ratification of the Conventions of nine States, shall be sufficient for the Establishment of this Constitution between the States so ratifying the Same. . . .

AMENDMENT I

Congress shall make no law respecting an establishment of religion, or prohibiting the free exercise thereof; or abridging the freedom of speech, or of the press; or the right of the people peaceably to assemble, and to petition the Government for a redress of grievances.

AMENDMENT II

A well regulated Militia, being necessary to the security of a free State, the right of the people to keep and bear Arms, shall not be infringed.

AMENDMENT III

No Soldier shall, in time of peace be quartered in any house, without the consent of the Owner, nor in time of war, but in a manner to be prescribed by law.

AMENDMENT IV

The right of the people to be secure in their persons, houses, papers, and effects, against unreasonable searches and seizures, shall not be violated, and no Warrants shall issue, but upon probable cause, supported by Oath or affirmation, and particularly decribing the place to be searched, and the persons or things to be seized.

AMENDMENT V

No person shall be held to answer for a capital, or otherwise infamous crime, unless on a presentment or indictment of a Grand Jury, except in cases arising in the land or naval forces, or in the Militia, when in actual service in time of War or public danger; nor shall any person be subject for the same offence to be twice put in jeopardy of life or limb; nor shall be compelled in any criminal case to be a witness against himself, nor be deprived of life, liberty, or property, without due process of law; nor shall private property be taken for public use, without just compensation.

AMENDMENT VI

In all criminal prosecutions, the accused shall enjoy the right to a speedy and public trial, by an impartial jury of the State and district wherein the crime shall have been committed, which district shall have been previously ascertained by law, and to be informed of the nature and cause of the accusation; to be confronted with the witnesses against him; to have compulsory process for obtaining witnesses in his favor, and to have the Assistance of Counsel for his defence.

AMENDMENT VII

In Suits at common law, where the value in controversy shall exceed twenty dollars, the right of trial by jury shall be preserved, and no fact tried by a jury, shall be otherwise re-examined in any Court of the United States, than according to the rules of the common law.

AMENDMENT VIII

Excessive bail shall not be required, nor excessive fines imposed, nor cruel and unusual punishments inflicted.

AMENDMENT IX

The enumeration in the Constitution, of certain rights, shall not be construed to deny or disparage others retained by the people.

AMENDMENT X

The powers not delegated to the United States by the Constitution, nor prohibited by it to the States, are reserved to the States respectively, or to the people.

AMENDMENT XI

The Judicial power of the United States shall not be construed to extend to any suit in law or equity, commenced or prosecuted against one of the United States by Citizens of another State, or by Citizens or Subjects of any Foreign State.

AMENDMENT XII

The Electors shall meet in their respective states and vote by ballot for President and Vice-President, one of whom, at least, shall not be an inhabitant of the same state with themselves; they shall name in their ballots the person voted for as

President, and in distinct ballots the person voted for as Vice-President, and they shall make distinct lists of all persons voted for as President, and of all persons voted for as Vice-President, and of the number of votes for each, which lists they shall sign and certify, and transmit sealed to the seat of the government of the United States, directed to the President of the Senate;—The President of the Senate shall, in the presence of the Senate and House of Representatives, open all the certificates and the votes shall then be counted;—The person having the greatest number of votes for President, shall be the President, if such number be a majority of the whole number of Electors appointed; and if no person have such majority, then from the persons having the highest numbers not exceeding three on the list of those voted for as President, the House of Representatives shall choose immediately, by ballot, the President. But in choosing the President, the votes shall be taken by states, the representation from each state having one vote; a quorum for this purpose shall consist of a member or members from two-thirds of the states, and a majority of all the states shall be necessary to a choice. And if the House of Representatives shall not choose a President whenever the right of choice shall devolve upon them, before the fourth day of March next following, then the Vice-President shall act as President, as in the case of the death or other constitutional disability of the President—The person having the greatest number of votes as Vice-President, shall be the Vice-President, if such number be a majority of the whole number of Electors appointed, and if no person have a majority, then from the two highest numbers on the list, the Senate shall choose the Vice-President; a quorum for the purpose shall consist of two-thirds of the whole number of Senators, and a majority of the whole number shall be necessary to a choice. But no person constitutionally ineligible to the office of President shall be eligible to that of Vice-President of the United States.

AMENDMENT XIII

Section 1. Neither slavery nor involuntary servitude, except as a punishment for crime whereof the party will have been duly convicted, shall exist within the United States, or any place subject to their jurisdiction.

Section 2. Congress shall have power to enforce this article by appropriate legislation.

Section 1. All persons born or naturalized in the United States and subject to the jurisdiction thereof, are citizens of the United States and of the State wherein they reside. No State shall make or enforce any law which shall abridge the privileges or immunities of citizens of the United States; or shall any State deprive any person of life, liberty, or property, without due process of law; nor deny to any person within its jurisdiction the equal protection of the laws.

Section 2. Representatives shall be apportioned among the several States according to their respective numbers, counting the whole number of persons in each State, excluding Indians not taxed. But when the right to vote at any election for the choice of electors for President and Vice President of the United States, Representatives in Congress, the Executive and Judicial officers of a State, or the members of the Legislature thereof, is denied to any of the male inhabitants of such State, being twenty-one years of age, and citizens of the United States, or in any way abridged, except for participation in rebellion, or other crime, the basis of representation therein shall be re- duced in the proportion which the number of such male citi- zens shall bear to the whole number of male citizens twenty one years of age in such State.

Section 3. No person shall be a Senator or Representative in Congress, or elector of President and Vice President, or hold any office, civil or military, under the United States, or under any State, who, having previously taken an oath, as a member of Congress, or as an officer of the United States, or as a member of any State legislature, or as an executive or judicial officer of any State, to support the Constitution of the United States, shall have engaged in insurrection or rebellion against the same, or given aid or comfort to the enemies thereof. But

Congress may by a vote of two-thirds of each House, remove such disability.

Section 4. The validity of the public debt of the United States, authorized by law, including debts incurred for payment of pensions and bounties for services in suppressing insurrection or rebellion, shall not be questioned. But neither the United States nor any State shall assume or pay any debt or obligation incurred in aid of insurrection or rebellion against the United States, or any claim for the loss or emancipation of any slave; but all such debts, obligations and claims shall be held illegal and void.

Section 5. The Congress shall have power to enforce, by appropriate legislation, the provisions of this article.

AMENDMENT XV

Section 1. The right of citizens of the United States to vote shall not be denied or abridged by the United States or by any State on account of race, color, or previous condition of servitude.

Section 2. The Congress shall have power to enforce this article by appropriate legislation.

AMENDMENT XVI

The Congress shall have power to lay and collect taxes on incomes, from whatever source derived, without apportionment among the several States, and without regard to any census or enumeration.

AMENDMENT XVII

The Senate of the United States shall be composed of two Senators from each State, elected by the people thereof, for six years; and each Senator shall have one vote. The electors in each State shall have the qualifications requisite for electors of the most numerous branch of the State legislatures.

When vacancies happen in the representation of any State in the Senate, the executive authority of such State shall issue writs of election to fill such vacancies: *Provided,* that the legislature of any State may empower the executive thereof to make temporary appointments until the people fill the vacancies by election as the legislature may direct.

This amendment shall not be so construed as to affect the election or term of any Senator chosen before it becomes valid as part of the Constitution.

AMENDMENT XVIII

Section 1. After one year from the ratification of this article the manufacture, sale, or transportation of intoxicating liquors within, the importation thereof into, or the exportation thereof from the United States and all territory subject to the jurisdiction thereof for beverage purposes is hereby prohibited.

Section 2. The Congress and the several States shall have concurrent power to enforce this article by appropriate legislation.

Section 3. This article shall be inoperative unless it shall have been ratified as an amendment to the Constitution by the legislatures of the several States, as provided in the Constitution, within seven years from the date of the submission hereof to the States by the Congress.

AMENDMENT XIX

The right of citizens of the United States to vote shall not be denied or abridged by the United States or by any State on account of sex.

Congress shall have power to enforce this article by appropriate legislation.

AMENDMENT XX

Section 1. The terms of the President and Vice President shall end at noon on the 20th day of January, and the terms of Senators and Representatives at noon on the 3rd day of January, of the years in which such terms would have ended if this article had not been ratified; and the terms of their successors shall then begin.

Section 2. The Congress shall assemble at least once in every year, and such meeting shall begin at noon on the 3rd day of January, unless they shall by law appoint a different day.

Section 3. If, at the time fixed for the beginning of the term of the President, the President elect shall have died, the Vice President elect shall become President. If a President shall not have been chosen before the time fixed for the beginning of his term, or if the President elect shall have failed to qualify, then the Vice President elect shall act as President until a President shall have qualified; and the Congress may by law provide for the case wherein neither a President elect nor a Vice President elect shall have qualified, declaring who shall then act as President, or the manner in which one who is to act shall be selected, and such person shall act accordingly until a President or Vice President shall have qualified.

Section 4. The Congress may by law provide for the case of the death of any of the persons from whom the House of Representatives may choose a President whenever the right of choice shall have devolved upon them, and for the case of the death of any of the persons from whom the Senate may choose a Vice President whenever the right of choice shall have devolved upon them.

Section 5. Sections 1 and 2 shall take effect on the 15th day of October following the ratification of this article.

Section 6. This article shall be inoperative unless it shall have been ratified as an amendment to the Constitution by the legislatures of three-fourths of the several States within seven years from the date of its submission.

AMENDMENT XXI

Section 1. The eighteenth article of amendment to the Constitution of the United States is hereby repealed.

Section 2. The transportation or importation into any State, Territory or possession of the United States for delivery or use therein of intoxicating liquors, in violation of the laws thereof, is hereby prohibited.

Section 3. This article shall be inoperative unless it shall have been ratified as an amendment to the Constitution by conventions in the several States, as provided in the Constitution, within seven years from the date of the submission hereof to the States by the Congress.

AMENDMENT XXII

Section 1. No person shall be elected to the office of the President more than twice, and no person who has held the office of President, or acted as President, for more than two years of a term to which some other person was elected President shall be elected to the office of the President more than once. But this article shall not apply to any person holding the office of President when this article was proposed by the Congress, and shall not prevent any person who may be holding the office of President, or acting as President, during the term within which this article becomes operative from holding the office of President or acting as President during the remainder of such term.

Section 2. This article shall be inoperative unless it shall have been ratified as an amendment to the Constitution by the legislatures of three-fourths of the several States within seven years from the date of its submission to the States by the Congress.

AMENDMENT XXIII

Section 1. The District constituting the seat of Government of the United States shall appoint in such manner as the Congress may direct:

A number of electors of President and Vice President equal to the whole number of Senators and Representatives in Congress to which the District would be entitled if it were a State, but in no event more than the least populous State; they shall be in addition to those appointed by the States, but they shall be considered, for the purposes of the election of President and Vice President, to be electors appointed by a State;

and they shall meet in the District and perform such duties as provided by the twelfth article of amendment.

Section 2. The Congress shall have power to enforce this article by appropriate legislation.

AMENDMENT XXIV

Section 1. The right of citizens of the United States to vote in any primary or other election for President or Vice President, for electors for President or Vice President, or for Senator or Representative in Congress, shall not be denied or abridged by the United States or any State by reason of failure to pay any poll tax or other tax.

Section 2. The Congress shall have power to enforce this article by appropriate legislation.

AMENDMENT XXV

Section 1. In case of the removal of the President from office or of his death or resignation, the Vice President shall become President.

Section 2. Whenever there is a vacancy in the office of the Vice President, the President shall nominate a Vice President who shall take office upon confirmation by a majority vote of both Houses of Congress.

Section 3. Whenever the President transmits to the President pro tempore of the Senate and the Speaker of the House of Representatives his written declaration that he is unable to discharge the powers and duties of his office, and until he transmits to them a written declaration to the contrary, such powers and duties shall be discharged by the Vice President as Acting President.

Section 4. Whenever the Vice President and a majority of either the principal officers of the executive departments or of such other body as Congress may by law provide, transmit to the President pro tempore of the Senate and the Speaker of the House of Representatives their written declaration that the President is unable to discharge the powers and duties of his office, the Vice President shall immediately assume the powers and duties of the office as Acting President.

Thereafter, when the President transmits to the President pro tempore of the Senate and the Speaker of the House of Representatives his written declaration that no inability exists, he shall resume the powers and duties of his office unless the Vice President and a majority of either the principal officers of the executive department or of such other body as Congress may by law provide, transmit within four days to the President pro tempore of the Senate and the Speaker of the House of Representatives their written declaration that the President is unable to discharge the powers and duties of his office. Thereupon Congress shall decide the issue, assembling within forty-eight hours for that purpose if not in session. If the Congress, within twenty-one days after receipt of the latter written declaration, or, if Congress is not in session, within twenty-one days after Congress is required to assemble, determines by two-thirds vote of both Houses that the President is unable to discharge the powers and duties of his office, the Vice President shall continue to discharge the same as Acting President; otherwise the President shall resume the powers and duties of his office.

AMENDMENT XXVI

Section 1. The right of citizens of the United States, who are eighteen years of age or older, to vote shall not be denied or abridged by the United States or by any State on account of age.

Section 2. The Congress shall have power to enforce this article by appropriate legislation.

Appendix B

The Associate Justices

NAME	PARTY & STATE APPOINTED FROM	TERM	NOMINATED BY
[John Jay]			
John Rutledge	Federalist—S.C.	1789–1791	Washington
William Cushing	Federalist—Mass.	1789–1810	Washington
James Wilson	Federalist—Pa.	1789–1798	Washington
John Blair	Federalist—Va.	1789–1796	Washington
James Iredell	Federalist—N.C.	1790–1799	Washington
Thomas Johnson	Federalist—Md.	1791–1793	Washington
William Paterson	Federalist—N.J.	1793–1806	Washington
[John Rutledge]			
Samuel Chase	Federalist—Md.	1796–1811	Washington
[Oliver Ellsworth]			
Bushrod Washington	Federalist—Va.	1798–1829	J. Adams
Alfred Moore	Federalist—N.C.	1799–1804	J. Adams
[John Marshall]			
William Johnson	Republican—S.C.	1804–1834	Jefferson
Henry Brockholst Livingston	Republican—N.Y.	1806–1823	Jefferson
Thomas Todd	Republican—Ky.	1807–1826	Jefferson
Joseph Story	Republican—Mass.	1811–1845	Madison
Gabriel Duval	Republican—Md.	1811–1835	Madison

NAME	PARTY & STATE APPOINTED FROM	TERM	NOMINATED BY
Smith Thompson	Republican—N.Y.	1823–1843	Monroe
Robert Trimble	Republican—Ky.	1826–1828	J. Q. Adams
John McLean	Democrat—Ohio	1829–1861	Jackson
Henry Baldwin	Democrat—Pa.	1830–1844	Jackson
James Moore Wayne	Democrat—Ga.	1835–1867	Jackson
[Roger B. Taney]			
Phillip Pendleton Barbour	Democrat—Va.	1836–1841	Jackson
John Catron	Democrat—Tenn.	1837–1865	Van Buren
John McKinley	Democrat—Ala.	1837–1852	Van Buren
Peter Vivian Daniel	Democrat—Va.	1841–1860	Van Buren
Samuel Nelson	Democrat—N.Y.	1845–1872	Tyler
Levi Woodbury	Democrat—N.H.	1845–1851	Polk
Robert Cooper Grier	Democrat—Pa.	1846–1870	Polk
Benjamin Robbins Curtis	Whig—Mass.	1851–1857	Fillmore
John Archibald Campbell	Democrat—Ala.	1853–1861	Pierce
Nathan Clifford	Democrat—Maine	1858–1881	Buchanan
Noah Haynes Swayne	Republican—Ohio	1862–1881	Lincoln
Samuel Freeman Miller	Republican—Iowa	1862–1890	Lincoln
David Davis	Republican—Ill. [later Democrat]	1862–1877	Lincoln
Stephen Johnson Field	Democrat—Calif.	1863–1897	Lincoln
[Salmon P. Chase]			
William Strong	Republican—Pa.	1870–1880	Grant
Joseph P. Bradley	Republican—N.J.	1870–1892	Grant
Ward Hunt	Republican—N.Y.	1873–1882	Grant
[Morrison R. Waite]			
John Marshall Harlan	Republican—Ky.	1877–1911	Hayes
William Burnham Woods	Republican—Ga.	1880–1887	Hayes
Stanley Matthews	Republican—Ohio	1881–1889	Garfield
Horace Gray	Republican—Mass.	1882–1902	Arthur
Samuel Blatchford	Republican—N.Y.	1882–1893	Arthur
Lucius Quintus C. Lamar	Democrat—Miss.	1888–1893	Cleveland
[Melville W. Fuller]			
David Josiah Brewer	Republican—Kansas	1889–1910	Harrison
Henry Billings Brown	Republican—Mich.	1890–1906	Harrison
George Shiras, Jr.	Republican—Pa.	1892–1903	Harrison
Howell Edmunds Jackson	Democrat—Tenn.	1893–1895	Harrison
Edward Douglass White	Democrat—La.	1894–1910	Cleveland
Rufus Wheeler Peckham	Democrat—N.Y.	1896–1909	Cleveland
Joseph McKenna	Republican—Calif.	1898–1925	McKinley
Oliver Wendell Holmes, Jr.	Republican—Mass.	1902–1932	T. Roosevelt
William Rufus Day	Republican—Ohio	1903–1922	T. Roosevelt
William Henry Moody	Republican—Mass.	1906–1910	T. Roosevelt
Horace Harmon Lurton	Democrat—Tenn.	1910–1914	Taft

NAME	PARTY & STATE APPOINTED FROM	TERM	NOMINATED BY
Charles Evans Hughes	Republican—N.Y.	1910–1916	Taft
Willis Van Devanter	Republican—Wyo.	1910–1937	Taft
Joseph Rucker Lamar	Democrat—Ga.	1911–1916	Taft
[Edward D. White]			
Mahlon Pitney	Republican—N.J.	1912–1922	Taft
James Clark McReynolds	Democrat—Tenn.	1914–1941	Wilson
Louis Dembitz Brandeis	Democrat—Mass.	1916–1939	Wilson
John Hessin Clarke	Democrat—Ohio	1916–1922	Wilson
[William H. Taft]			
George Sutherland	Republican—Utah	1922–1938	Harding
Pierce Butler	Democrat—Minn.	1923–1939	Harding
Edward Terry Sanford	Republican—Tenn.	1923–1930	Harding
Harlan Fiske Stone	Republican—N.Y.	1925–1941	Coolidge
[Charles E. Hughes]			
Owen Josephus Roberts	Republican—Pa.	1930–1945	Hoover
Benjamin Nathan Cardozo	Democrat—N.Y.	1932–1938	Hoover
Hugo Lafayette Black	Democrat—Ala.	1937–1971	F. D. Roosevelt
Stanley Forman Reed	Democrat—Ky.	1938–1957	F. D. Roosevelt
Felix Frankfurter	Independent—Mass. [Democrat]	1939–1962	F. D. Roosevelt
William Orville Douglas	Democrat—Conn.	1939–1975	F. D. Roosevelt
Frank Murphy	Democrat—Mich.	1940–1949	F. D. Roosevelt
[Harlan F. Stone]			
James Francis Byrnes	Democrat—S.C.	1941–1942	F. D. Roosevelt
Robert Houghwout Jackson	Democrat—N.Y.	1941–1954	F. D. Roosevelt
Wiley Blount Rutledge	Democrat—Iowa	1943–1949	F. D. Roosevelt
Harold Hitz Burton	Republican—Ohio	1945–1958	Truman
[Fred M. Vinson]			
Thomas Campbell Clark	Democrat—Texas	1949–1967	Truman
Sherman Minton	Democrat—Ind.	1949–1956	Truman
[Earl Warren]			
John Marshall Harlan	Republican—N.Y.	1955–1971	Eisenhower
William Joseph Brennan, Jr.	Democrat—N.J.	1956–	Eisenhower
Charles Evans Whittaker	Republican—Mo.	1957–1962	Eisenhower
Potter Stewart	Republican—Ohio	1958–	Eisenhower
Byron Raymond White	Democrat—Colo.	1962–	Kennedy
Arthur Joseph Goldberg	Democrat—Ill.	1962–1965	Kennedy
Abe Fortas	Democrat—Tenn.	1965–1969	Johnson
Thurgood Marshall	Democrat—N.Y.	1967–	Johnson
[Warren E. Burger]			
Harry Andrew Blackmun	Republican—Minn.	1970–	Nixon
Lewis Franklin Powell, Jr.	Democrat—Va.	1972–	Nixon
William Hubbs Rehnquist	Republican—Ariz.	1972–	Nixon
John Paul Stevens	Republican—Ill.	1975–	Ford

Bibliography

It has been my aim to compile a detailed yet clear guide to the Supreme Court of the United States for the young reader. From various sources, I have gathered vital facts and statistics about the Court's purpose, background, and accomplishments during its almost two-hundred-year history. In order to investigate the growth and development of the Supreme Court, I have supplemented my own knowledge by consulting many books, encyclopedias, magazines, newspapers, pamphlets, and articles. The following list does not include all my sources; it is offered here as additional reading material that will benefit those who may desire to pursue the subject further.

Alfange, Dean, *The Supreme Court and the National Will* (New York: Doubleday, Doran, 1937).

Carr, Robert K., *The Supreme Court and Judicial Review* (New York: Farrar & Rinehart, 1942).

Current Biography (New York: H. W. Wilson, 1941, 1943, 1969).

Dictionary of American Biography (New York: Charles Scribner's Sons, 1931, 1933, 1936).

Habenstreit, Barbara, *Changing America and the Supreme Court* (New York: Julian Messner, 1974).

Haines, Charles G., and Sherwood, Foster H., *The Role of the Supreme Court in American Government and Politics, 1835–1864* (Berkeley and Los Angeles: University of California Press, 1957).

Hart, Albert B., *Salmon Portland Chase* (New York: Greenwood Press, 1969).

Hendel, Samuel, *Charles Evans Hughes and the Supreme Court* (New York: King's Crown Press, Columbia University, 1951).

Jackson, Percival E., *Dissent in the Supreme Court—a Chronology* (Norman, Oklahoma: University of Oklahoma Press, 1969).

————, ed., *The Wisdom of the Supreme Court* (Norman, Oklahoma: University of Oklahoma Press, 1962).

Katz, William L., and Gaughran, Bernard, *The Constitutional Amendments* (New York: Franklin Watts, 1974).

Latham, Frank F., *American Justice on Trial* (New York: Franklin Watts, 1972).

Lieberman, Jethro K., *Court in Session* (New York: Sterling Publishing, 1966).

Loth, David, *Chief Justice John Marshall and the Growth of the Republic* (New York: W. W. Norton, 1949).

McCloskey, Robert G., *The American Supreme Court* (Chicago: University of Chicago Press, 1960).

Mason, Alpheus T., *Harlan Fiske Stone: Pillar of the Law* (New York: Viking Press, 1956).

————, *The Supreme Court from Taft to Warren* (Baton Rouge: Louisiana State University Press, 1958).

Monaghan, Frank, *John Jay, Defender of Liberty* (New York and Indianapolis: Bobbs-Merrill, 1935).

Morris, Richard B., ed., *Encyclopedia of American History* (New York: Harper & Row, 1965).

————, *The First Book of the Constitution* (New York: Franklin Watts, 1958).

Salomon, Leon I., ed., *The Supreme Court* (New York: H. W. Wilson, 1961).

Saylor, Richard H.; Boyer, Barry B.; and Gooding, Robert E., Jr., *The Warren Court: A Critical Analysis* (New York: Chelsea House, 1968).

Steinberg, Alfred, *John Marshall* (New York: G. P. Putnam's Sons, 1962).

Swindler, William F., *Court and Constitution in the 20th Century: The Old Legality, 1889–1932* (Indianapolis and New York: Bobbs-Merrill, 1969).

————, *Court and Constitution in the 20th Century: The New Legality, 1932–1968* (Indianapolis and New York: Bobbs-Merrill, 1970).

————, *Court and Constitution in the 20th Century: The Modern Interpretation* (Indianapolis and New York: Bobbs-Merrill, 1974).

Tresolini, Rocco J., *Justice and the Supreme Court* (Philadelphia and New York: J. B. Lippincott, 1963).

Whitelock, William, *The Life and Times of John Jay* (New York: Dodd, Mead, 1887).

The World Almanac and Book of Facts (New York and Cleveland: Newspaper Enterprise Association, 1971, 1972, 1973, 1974, 1975).

For more detailed information about the United States Supreme Court and its decisions, two excellent sources, *The Harvard Law Review* and the *United States Reports*, are recommended.

I am indebted to my Congressman and to many others for their prompt replies to my letters of inquiry. I owe special thanks to the Office of the Marshal of the Supreme Court, the Public Information Office of the Supreme Court of the United States, and the United States Government Printing Office for making relevant data available to me.

I am indeed grateful to many—writers, editors, and others—for abundant and expert help in the preparation of this book.

Quincy, Illinois   Dorothy A. Marquardt

Glossary

Amendment—Generally, the term "amendment" means a later addition to or change in a document or statement. The United States Constitution has had added to it twenty-six amendments, each of which, when finally passed, became a part of the Constitution, with as much force and effect as the original document has. Article V of the Constitution sets forth the method to be used to amend the Constitution.

Bill of Rights—This is the term generally used to refer to the first ten amendments to the Constitution. These amendments were not a part of the original Constitution; they were added, all at the same time, shortly after the original document was adopted. The first eight amendments contained in the Bill of Rights deal with certain specified rights and privileges of citizens of the United States. The Ninth Amendment states that the fact that a right is not dealt with in the first eight amendments should not be interpreted to mean that citizens do not have such a right. The Tenth Amendment attempts to reserve for the states and the citizens those powers not specifically granted to the federal government.

Certiorari, writ of—This is the formal name for the decision of the Supreme Court of the United States to review a determination of a lower court. Not all cases are entitled to an automatic appeal to the Supreme Court. In those cases which are not automatically appealable, the party wishing to appeal must petition the Supreme Court for a writ of certiorari. Only if the Supreme Court agrees, by granting the writ, is the party able to make his appeal. Otherwise, the decision of the lower court must stand.

Conscientious Objectors—This term refers to those persons who, because of their moral or religious beliefs, are excused by law from the performance of compulsory military service.

Defamation—Defamation is the wrongful making of statements that damage the reputation of a person in the community.

Desegregation—This term generally refers to the process of eliminating illegal patterns of separating persons on the basis of race. It describes, for example, the process of ending the illegal separation of students into all-black and all-white schools.

Discrimination—Generally, this term means the act of distinguishing between things of different kind or quality. In the context of Supreme Court decisions, the term "discrimination" refers to the denial of rights or privileges to a person or persons by reason of the person's or persons' race, religion, national origin, sex or age.

Docket—A court's docket is the group of cases filed with the court and awaiting action by the court.

Double Jeopardy—The Fifth Amendment to the U.S. Constitution provides that no person shall "be subject for the same offense to be twice put in jeopardy of life or limb." This means that if the proceeding against a person charged with committing a crime has reached a certain stage and then is discontinued in a given way, criminal charges cannot again be brought against that person for the same act that gave rise to the first charge. A complicated body of law has been built up in this area, but the basic rule is that once a charge has been decided on or disposed of, the decision or disposition is final.

Due Process—This term refers to the rights of citizens to have institutions and procedures for the determination and protection of their rights and privileges under the law, and to have those institutions and procedures designed and administered in such a way as to provide not just the form but also the substance of fair determination and adequate protection of rights and privileges.

Equal Protection—This term is taken from a phrase in the Fourteenth Amendment that forbids any state to "deny to any person within its jurisdiction the equal protection of the laws." Simply stated, it means that the laws are to be enforced and interpreted impartially, and that the rights and privileges of citizens under the law are to be available to all citizens, without favoritism for any person or class of people.

Felony—Crimes are generally divided into two categories, "misdemeanors" and "felonies." A misdemeanor is a less serious crime, such as disorderly conduct, usually punishable by a fine and, sometimes, a relatively short prison sentence. Felonies are the more serious types of crime, such as robbery, embezzlement, and kidnapping, generally punishable by much longer prison sentences.

Impeachment—This is a process by which a President or a Justice of the Supreme Court is formally charged with misconduct for which, if he is convicted, he may be removed from office. Impeachment does not mean removal from office, but only the bringing of charges that might lead ultimately to removal.

Infringe—This refers to an act by one person that is inconsistent with and preventative of the full exercise by another person of certain of his rights or privileges. The rights infringed upon may be artificially created rights, such as the right to the exclusive use of a patent. On the other hand, they may be fundamental rights, such as the right to free speech.

Majority Opinion—The vote of a majority of the members of the Supreme Court is required for a decision on a case. When the Justices who are in the majority are in agreement on the legal reasons for their decision, one of the members of the majority will write a legal opinion on their behalf, setting forth their reasoning. There are times when a Justice who is in the majority agrees with the result reached by the other members of the majority, but disagrees with the reasons for which the other members of the majority voted that way. In such a case, the Justice will often write a concurring opinion setting forth the reasons why he voted with the other Justices in the majority. Similarly, a Justice who is in the minority may deliver a dissenting opinion setting forth the reasons why he disagrees with the majority.

Monopoly—This term refers to the situation in a particular industry when one company in that industry has virtually eliminated all competition and is able to control the supply and price of goods or services.

Original Jurisdiction—Most cases decided by the Supreme Court come before the court by way of appeal from a lower court. The Court's power to decide these cases is referred to as "appellate jurisdiction." There are, however, a few kinds of cases that originate with the Supreme Court, and not with a lower court in the federal system or with a state court. The Supreme Court is said to have "original jurisdiction" with respect to these types of cases. Cases in which the Supreme Court may exercise original jurisdiction are specified in Article III of the Constitution.

Prior Restraint—This term, used (as it most often is) in the context of decisions relating to freedom of speech under the First Amendment to the Constitution, refers to the prevention of the exercise of a form of speech or expression prior to such exercise, as opposed to either the punishment of a person who wrongfully exercises the form of speech or expression, or the prohibition of further exercise of the speech or expression after it has once been exercised.

Search Warrant—This is an order issued by a court, permitting the police to search an individual's person, residence, or other possessions. The place to be searched must be stated in the warrant, and the search may not go beyond the place specified. The warrant is issued by the court only after the judge has decided that the reasons for the search outweigh the right to privacy of the individual who is the subject of the search.

Self-Incrimination—This term refers to a person's giving evidence that he himself has committed a crime. The Fifth Amendment to the Constitution provides that no individual may be required to give evidence against himself.

Stare Decisis—This is a Latin phrase referring to the legal doctrine that once a court has decided a point of law, that court and all courts which are junior to that court—*i.e.*, all courts from which an appeal may be taken to that court—should be bound by the decision of the higher court on that point of law and should decide subsequent cases involving that point of law in a consistent manner.

Index